MORE PRAISE FOR **DATING YOUR MONEY**

"Dress up, stand tall, look your money straight in the eye, and connect. JENNIFER WILKOV takes you by the hand and leads you effortlessly through 8 easy steps to having a successful relationship with your money. Get ready to date your money!"

—LAUREN SOLOMON, author of **IMAGE MATTERS!**
FIRST STEPS ON THE JOURNEY TO YOUR BEST SELF

"DATING YOUR MONEY goes straight to the heart of money matters. Read the book to begin a spectacular relationship with your money today."

—KEITH J. CUNNINGHAM, author of **KEYS TO THE VAULT**

"DATING YOUR MONEY is a fun and fresh approach to improving your relationship with money. The book is written in simple no-nonsense language, and I recommend you purchase two copies: one for yourself and one for a loved one!"

—ALEX MANDOSSIAN, CEO & founder of Heritage House Publishing, Inc.

"Money is a basic part of daily existence. Most of us see it as something lifeless–to be used, hoarded, or worried about. JENNIFER-SAN brings money to life, and makes finances an organic part of our journey. I recommend this book to anyone who wants to know money better and worry about it less."

—H.F. ITO, master shintaido instructor

"JENNIFER WILKOV is a gifted financial advisor whose advice comes from the heart. While taking you down the path of green energy, JENNIFER focuses on making happiness. I recommend this book highly for those who not only want to make a million but also want to make a life."

—SENSEI DON CARDOZA, director of the Wellness Resource Center

"DATING YOUR MONEY has taught me what I have been missing. The approach gives a whole new meaning to money: It shows you how to take care of your money . . . and to let your finances take care of you. Women will find this book irresistible!"

—HESHIE SEGAL, founder of the Girlfriend Connection
and JetNetting Connection

Dating Your Money

How to Build a Long-Lasting Relationship with Your Money in **8** Easy Steps

by **Jennifer S. Wilkov, CFP®**

Published by E.S.P. Press Corp.
A division of Evolutionary Strategic Planning, Inc.
189 Montague Street, Ste 900, Brooklyn, NY 11201, USA

Dating Your Money by Jennifer S. Wilkov
Copyright © 2006 E.S.P. Press Corp.
All Rights Reserved.

Cover and text design: **Keith Graphics, llc**
Illustrations: **Julia Durgee**

Printed in Mexico by R.R. Donnelley
First printing February 2006

ISBN 0-9777347-0-6

♥ Dedication ♥

For you, dear reader:

Thank you for your generosity of spirit and for the trust you have placed in me by seeking the guidance provided in this book.

May the information in **DATING YOUR MONEY** contribute to your everlasting loving relationship with money and may it enrich the lives of those with whom you share your heart's desires and dreams.

I wish you love and money.

Jennifer

Acknowledgments

Books come to life through a series of small miracles and passionate work. In this case, many people have devoted vision, a lot of energy, time, and the sharing of ideas to bring this work to you, dear reader. My own personal inspiration, insight, and experience also provided me with the encouragement to realize DATING YOUR MONEY.

I am grateful each day for the divine loving guidance I feel in my life. My family has been very supportive through this effort, and I want to thank them individually for their love, kindness, and generosity: my nieces, Logan, age 2 $^1/_2$, and Sydney Rachel, age 6; my parents; my brother, Jeffrey; and my grandmothers, Charlotte, age 87, and Fay, 90. Each one found a unique way to cheer me on during my foray into how to write a book in ninety days! Thank you for being who you are, and for sharing your money relationships with me.

Many thanks to my clients — from whom I continue to learn so much: You are an amazing group of individuals and couples, and I am blessed by your generosity of spirit and willingness to seek financial advice and assistance. Thank you for supporting me as I reach out for one of my dreams — the publication of DATING YOUR MONEY.

I also have a special group of people who continue to bless my life. I want to thank them too: my mentors and friends in the worlds of personal growth, academia, and the martial arts of Shintaido and Aikido. I have incredible love, admiration, respect, and gratitude for many individuals and mentors who have come serendipitously into my life: Anthony Robbins; Mark Victor Hansen; Robert G. Allen; T. Harv Eker; Joel and Heidi Wall Roberts; Lauren Solomon; Blair Singer; Keith Cunningham; Alex Mandossian; R. Buckminster Fuller; H. F. Ito, Sensei; Don Cardoza, Sensei; Toshimitsu Ishii, Sensei; David Franklin, Sensei; Mishashi Minagawa, Sensei; and others. Thank you for supporting me and continuing to inspire me as I enjoy my life's work.

I applaud the outstanding people in my company, Evolutionary Strategic Planning (E.S.P.), specifically, Eileen Bonilla and Schonda Fields: They have incredibly generous hearts. These two talented women have also been right alongside me in the journey of this book. They support me in a way that no one else can: They assist me daily in keeping my own multiple sources of income flowing so I can focus on new projects!

My championship team consists of individuals who want more for me than I have ever imagined for myself. It is an honor and privilege to have each of you in my life. I thank you for your commitment to my success — and your contribution to my life experiences. Your faith, love, and support are unending. Thank you for being in my life.

Here are a few of the names of the many talented individuals on my championship team: David Halperin of Halperin & Halperin P.C.; Alan Sutin and Jessica Turko from Greenberg Traurig; and my brilliant publishing team includes: Liz Walker of Walker Publishing Services Inc., who brought together an amazing group of people to work on this project. Liz guided and assisted me in gaining a deeper understanding of the mechanics of publishing, and she has managed the project with incredible aplomb. Roberta Fineberg of A Muse Productions brought her rewriting and editorial expertise to bear on what has become an awesome manuscript. I appreciate her extra efforts and generous contributions to making DATING YOUR MONEY a top-flight book. Parlan McGaw of Golden Arts & Letters has lent his eagle-eyed copyediting skills to the project: It has been a joy to work with and learn from him. Keith Conover of K. Graphics LLC has been enormously successful in translating the spirit of the book in his layout and design. Watching how he treats the themes of the book in his design work has truly been a delight — I appreciate the visual masterpiece he has created! Julia Durgee, young illustrator extraordinaire, contributes her prodigious talents to her first book project. It has been exciting to witness her inspirational interpretations of the text: Thank you for your creativity and talent, and for making the book — my wonderful gift to the world — possible.

Last but not least, I want to take a moment to acknowledge the reader. I admire and applaud your courage to seek guidance and information to reach your goals. I am an enthusiastic partner in your success plan — proactive in helping you build your relationship with money. Thank you for trusting me.

In closing, I share one of the epiphanies I experienced while collaborating on the book. As I wanted to produce a book that everyone could read and understand — and could use the information promptly to transform her relationship with money — I struggled with the pronoun problem of masculine and feminine. In the end I opted for the feminine pronoun, and use it throughout the book. Please accept my apology in paying more attention to women's relationships with money. However, my intention is to offer all readers a simple system for creating and sustaining a relationship with money. The confines of the English language aside, I believe anyone — female or male — can derive benefit from reading this book, which takes you by the hand on a step-by-step journey and guides you on a clear path to enjoying your infinite wealth.

ENJOY!

❤ Contents ❤

FOREWORD

Why do you want to have a relationship with your money?

If you think a financial planner is a middle-aged man with slicked-back hair who lugs around a fifty-pound computer bag and is on a mission to sell you his firm's latest products….Well, you wouldn't be thinking of me. I'm not just a financial planner, I'm a financial **pioneer**. I utilize the skills and services of a traditional financial planner, and I go light-years beyond in a revolutionary approach to how clients should be served.

As I moved up through the ranks of strategic planning and business development in Fortune 500 companies, I gained insight and experience through my work with colleagues. I marveled at their job choices and the sacrifices they made to support themselves and their families. I learned a lot about what people value in their lives— and it made me question my values and myself. After climbing the corporate ladders of many of the nation's top businesses for fourteen years, I ventured out on my own.

A key moment occurred one day while I was sitting in a late afternoon meeting with a senior executive at Liz Claiborne. I was a consultant for a business intelligence company, and the client had scheduled our meeting for 5:30 p.m. At the outset of the meeting, he stated that his son's baseball game was starting at the same time as our meeting. I looked at him and offered spontaneously that we could postpone our meeting until the morning if he wanted to get going for the game. The client gazed incredulously at me, smiled, and said: "Let's continue with the agenda."

Right then and there, I understood that my client was making a decision between being with his son at the game that night or continuing to work to support his family. Sacrificing the joy of spending time with his family for getting the job done, my client had made a monumental decision — yet he was unaware of it because his assumption was that he had no choice.

This was a big lesson for me because it made me think that there had to be a better way. There had to be a means for people to enjoy spending time with loved ones while still making enough money to support their families.

I carried this lesson into the world of financial planning, while learning the traditional methods of working with clients and their money. What I found was that the focus of clients was exclusively on money and not on their lifestyles. Money, alone, remained at the center of all financial discussions—how particular investments performed, where to find the biggest gains at the least risk to the client, and what companies were staying in business for the long haul.

The connection between what the clients wanted in their lives and how they felt about their money was lost because the company I was working for provided limited options for discussing feelings in financial planning. The limitations were imposed by the firm, which didn't encourage my work with clients' feelings around money. What was available was information about investment choices. These constraints troubled me as I explored investment possibilities with my clients and their money. My firm frowned on my approach because it only saw value in—and only compensated me for—what I sold, and not for the information, expertise, and guidance I shared with clients.

My experience showed me that firms wanted me to focus on the no-nonsense side of what clients wanted their money to do for them and their families. Positioning clients so that they first explored their financial situations and feelings about money seemed healthier to me when building a foundation for their relationship to wealth. Fostering my clients' relationships with their money is primarily what interested me, and it became my mission.

MONEY, MONEY, MONEY

We, as unique individuals, define and give meaning to our relationships with people and money. No one ever explained this simple concept to me. I learned it firsthand from my own experiences in the industry and by observing the behavior of my clients, like the Liz Claiborne executive, who made choices based on making money instead of spending time with the people in their lives.

Taking care of your money is similar to nurturing a child, cultivating a relationship with a significant other, or being responsible to a pet. Being attentive requires time, attention, energy, and effort to keep a relationship growing.

Year after year, I change, as does the world around me. I wear different clothes, try new hairstyles, move furniture around in my apartment—I transform my life and my environment. Likewise, requirements for my money change, too. What often happens is that people become so caught up in life that they literally lose sight of their money. Where your income is generated, what you choose to spend your cash on, and how you save and invest your monies often get lost in the shuffle of life. Pretty soon if we don't watch out, our money starts acting like a stranger! Then we have to get to know what our relationships to money are all over again.

By experiencing my own financial disasters I learned about money the hard way—and found that when I paid attention to my money on a regular basis, it actually grew with me. The regimen of getting your financial life in shape feels a little like going to the gym—the more you exercise with your money, the better results you get. It has been exciting to exercise a little muscle in helping people create positive money relationships in their lives. But most important, I share with you this: Your relationship with finances is simply a reflection of your life at the present time.

For my clients' lives and mine, I have been exploring a unique approach to money. In DATING YOUR MONEY you learn to share a deep understanding and appreciation of money by following the eight simple steps in the book. You will increase your knowledge and experience of money. And the time you spend working with it will become easier as you become more proficient at managing your financial life. Instead of obsessing and worrying about your money, you will have more time to spend with your family, friends, and colleagues without losing your connection to your finances. Now money has a purpose beyond quantitative value!

Time and Energy Are Investments Too

From my experience in the corporate world and now in my own practice, I guarantee that solid relationships are the keys to successful lives.

Your heart leads relationships. When you are interested in learning more about something or someone, you need to invest time and energy to accomplish the goal of having a rewarding and satisfying experience. When your heart leaps with excitement when you see the person you love, you want to spend more time with him or her because you enjoy the individual.

Creating a relationship and defining it is the cornerstone to building a successful connection. The possibilities of building alliances exist everywhere and with everyone—the people you choose to be with, the places you choose to live, and what you choose to do with your time each day. **Opportunities to grow are everywhere: delight in and honor your relationship with your money!**

Relationship Investments

Relationships involve four main factors, which encourage our learning and growth:

The Mind

Our desire to learn and know more about our relationships and the world is universal. When I am with someone who knows more than I do about a particular subject or person, I want to invest more time in being with him or her because I enjoy the knowledge and information the individual shares. When I know more about a subject, I share it with others around me. When you want to know more about a subject or a person, do you invest the time? This is also the case with our money. If you want to understand your finances better, you have to spend time doing research.

When I want to know more about my money, I read a book or talk to someone with financial expertise. I want to know how to evaluate my finances so that I can understand my money better. Investments of time and energy are based on interest. Do you want to get to know your money?

The Heart

Our hearts register feelings and emotions: exhilaration, delight, happiness, disappointment, sadness, anger, fear, and anxiety. Are emotions a result of our thoughts or are they spontaneous reactions? I feel happy, so I smile. I feel sad, so I cry. I feel mad, so I shout. Regardless of age, we experience a myriad of emotions as we gather information on life and different experiences. And with my money, I have a variety of feelings each time I discover new information about my finances.

I feel anxious when I don't have the information I need to be better informed about my investments. I feel happy when I receive money, spend money on something I enjoy, or give money to a charity to assist others. I feel sad when I don't know where my money has gone and feel deprived if there isn't enough money to go around. I feel angry when I expect my stocks to increase in value but they decline instead. Our money relationships are supercharged with emotions—so don't feel zapped!

The Soul

Our souls experience a union with God or a higher power that provides guidance, light, and support as we in turn reach out to others. I appreciate beauty, grace, and elegance in the world and in people. Feeling inspired by the world and people, I connect and contribute to the world community so everybody grows—together. The spiritual interrelationship of people and the environment pervades every area of my life too, including my money domain. My finances are not only about personal gain but also about responsibility to use resources to help other people on the planet.

Why do I want money? What does money represent in my life? How do I produce enough capital to benefit the world around me?

My mantra: I love what I do for my money, and I love what my money does for the world community and me.

The Body

Our bodies relate to the physical world, through the five senses: sight, touch, hearing, smell, and taste. The senses are delighted by tangible physical experiences, such as looking into the eyes of a lover or holding hands with a friend. Money is tangible too—you hold it in your hand, you track it in your accounts, you purchase objects you love for the home, you take it out of your wallet to buy clothes, you gladly use it to pay for the foods you eat, etc. Your money and you have a physical relationship!

These four facets—mind, heart, soul, and body—are in a dance of deep and satisfying connection. When one component is not present, relationships with people—and money—fall flat.

DATING YOUR MONEY

Who is this book for? It is for you—the woman who wants a fulfilling relationship with her money. You may be single, married, or divorced; you may or may not have children; you may have your own business or want to start one… You want someone to assist you in understanding your money, how it works for you and what to do with it when your relationship with money isn't working. You want to know how to protect it while breaking through fears and emotions around money. You ask: How do I create and sustain a relationship with my money? Read on!

1. Building a Relationship. Accept that you already have a money relationship. Then find out what you've been basing your relationships on in the past, let go of preconceived ideas, and get ready to create a fresh relationship with your money.

2. Making a Commitment. Create a long-lasting relationship with your money by making a commitment to yourself and your money. Become aware of your emotions and honor them so that you stay with your money in the relationship.

3. **Keeping a Commitment.** Check in with your feelings, and make sure you're getting the support you want in your relationship with money. Examine what works in your life and finances. What isn't working? What do you want to change? Celebrate both your consistent and inconsistent commitments. When you are inconsistent, find what doesn't work and make adjustments!

4. **Communicating and Connecting with Your Money.** How do you communicate with money: online, e-mail, by phone, or the old-fashioned way...? Set up a simple routine to spend quality time with your cash.

5. **Organizing Your Money.** Organize and manage your resources to see how the various parts of your financial reality intersect. It will be fast and easy for you to understand—promise!

6. **Dating Your Money**™. Let's get to it! In eight minutes a week, learn what to do with your quality time to nurture your money relationship. It's fun when you know how to do it!

7. **Taking a Money Time-Out**™. Take a holiday from your money to get a perspective—then start again fresh on your money relationship, knowing better what you want out of life.

8. **Embracing Change.** Use the DATING YOUR MONEY™ framework to keep the relationship full of life—and get a terrific return on your investment!

EIGHT MINUTES?

In Japanese culture and in feng shui, the number eight represents unlimited fortune. I have purposely created eight steps so you too may enjoy your own unlimited fortune.

In the beginning of your study, you will need to invest more than eight minutes to learn the first steps to prepare you to practice the eight-minutes-a-week program. When you learn the steps, you will create a quality relationship with your money in eight minutes a week. Also, you will learn to take a time-out to get a clear perspective on how to continually cultivate your money relationship. In eight simple steps everything you want is within your reach.

Five words of practical wisdom: Be well and be prosperous!

Congratulations

on becoming a certified
MONEY DATING ARCHITECT™!

Each week you work passionately
with your money because
you love what you do for your money...
and you love what it does for you!

Celebrate DATING YOUR MONEY™ success!

Jennifer S. Wilkov
_____   _____

Jennifer S. Wilkov, CFP®
Author of **DATING YOUR MONEY**

❤ MDA Certificate: Celebrate DATING YOUR MONEY™ SUCCESS ❤

[She] who cherishes a beautiful vision, a lofty ideal in [her] heart will one day realize it.   —James Allen
(from **As a Man Thinketh**)

Anyone can have a fulfilling and successful relationship with money. You are about to embark upon a journey of learning how to build a long-lasting relationship with money.

The eight steps begin with a desire to enjoy a positive relationship with your money. Throughout the journey, you will measure your progress and see your relationship to money transform as you complete each step. Your goal: To work with the building blocks and tools in each section to effectively organize your financial information. The result: you become a MONEY DATING ARCHITECT™!

To keep it simple and grow your relationship with money, I offer several resources to support you in your quest. Go to www.DatingYourMoney.com to register for the user-friendly forms, free special reports, and other assistance. At the end of each step, return to the website and make note of your progress.

Stay on board the DATING YOUR MONEY™ system and enjoy the program! When you have completed all eight steps, you will qualify to receive your MONEY DATING ARCHITECT™ CERTIFICATE OF ACHIEVEMENT!

Welcome!
Your successful relationship with money begins here…

Chapter 1

Looking for a long-lasting relationship...

Looking for a long-lasting relationship

Looking for a commitment

Looking for a supportive relationship

Looking for a good communicator

Looking for someone easy to spot in a crowd

Looking for someone who knows what they want from life and is willing to do whatever it takes to get it.

Looking for someone to grow with

I need a vacation...

Looking for a good communicator

Looking for someone easy to spot in a crowd

Looking for someone who knows what they want from life and is willing to do whatever it takes to get it.

Looking for someone to grow with

Looking for a commitment

Looking for a supportive relationship

Looking for a good communicator

Looking for someone easy to spot in a crowd.

I need a vacation!

Looking for someone to grow with

Looking for a commitment

Looking for a supportive relationship

Looking for a good communicator

Looking for someone easy to spot in a crowd.

Looking for someone who knows what they want from life and is willing to do whatever it takes to get it.

Looking for someone easy to spot in a crowd.

I need a vacation...

Looking for someone to grow with

Looking for a

someone who knows what they want from life and is willing to do whatever it takes to get it

Looking for someone to grow with

Looking for a long-lasting relationship

Looking for a commitment

Looking for a supportive relationship

Looking for a good communicator

Looking for someone easy to spot in a crowd

Looking for someone who knows what they want from life and is willing to do whatever it takes to get it.

Looking for a long-lasting relationship

Looking for a commitment

Looking for a supportive relationship

Looking for a good communicator

Looking for someone easy to spot in a crowd.

someone to grow with

Change

Looking for a long-lasting relationship

Looking for a commitment

Looking for a supportive relationship

Looking for a good communicator

Looking for someone easy to spot in a crowd

Looking for someone who knows what they want from

Looking for a long-lasting relationship

Looking for a commitment

Looking for a supportive relationship

Looking for

Looking for a long-lasting relationship

Looking for a commitment

Looking for a supportive relationship

Looking for a good communicator

Looking for someone easy to spot in a crowd

Looking for someone who knows what they want from life and is willing to do whatever it takes to get it.

Looking for someone to grow with

Looking for a long-lasting relationship

Looking for a commitment

Looking for a supportive relationship

I need a vacation...

Looking for someone easy to spot in

Why do I keep dating the same guys over and over again?

Building a Relationship

The sun rises in the east: It's a new day. You get up, ready to start your day. You feel refreshed and prepared to experience what life is going to offer. You ask yourself: "What do I want my day to be like?" Will the day turn out like the one you had the day before, or will it be different? Do you find that you often repeat events from last week, last month, last year?

Think for a moment: Do you want to build more positive relationships in your life?

Building more positive relationships means you want something different from what you have experienced already. Does this extend to your financial life too? Let's examine what you want to change in your life . . . and in your finances too.

That's right—you are in a relationship with your money. And you may not be aware that you are…until now. In the first step of DATING YOUR MONEY™ you take a close look at your money and examine what you want to change in your relationship with it.

Are you ready for a new relationship with finances?

Consider this: Is it possible for a person to create new meaning in life if she is unable to let go of the past and open herself up to fresh insights? A positive relationship means you are open to new experiences in your life. Get ready for a new outlook on your life and money.

In the first step of DATING YOUR MONEY™ you will learn to take a close look at your money, take stock of what you enjoy in life, and examine what you want to change about yourself. You will let go of destructive economic setbacks and be ready for a new relationship with your money.

YOUR MONEY HERITAGE

As the saying goes, history has a way of repeating itself.
Have you had two—maybe three—relationships in a row that
ended in the same way? Have you ever scratched your head
and asked: "Why do I keep meeting the same types of people
over and over again in my life?" Do you attract them? Are they
attracted to you?

How many times have you been out on a date and felt you
were like Bill Murray in the movie **Groundhog Day**? In the film,
Bill Murray was very frustrated because he repeated the same
experiences in the same places with the same people every
day. No matter what he tried to do differently in his life, he
kept reliving an identical day. In short, he was stuck.

This phenomenon happens in our financial lives, too. Like
the Bill Murray character, we're always working to get our lives
right—including our relationship with money. When you play
with your cash and credit cards like a yo-yo, you're **in the black**
one day and then in the red the next. Your relationship with
money provides clues about the way you have chosen to live
your life.

**If you want to change your relationship with your money,
YOU need to change.**

Let's take a look at your past and present relationship with
your money. Your money has its own family tree, which reveals
when your relationship with money started. This is called your
MONEY HERITAGE TREE™. Family, friends, teachers, and strangers
influence your money relationship. You may have already
noticed that people in your life exhibit different behaviors and

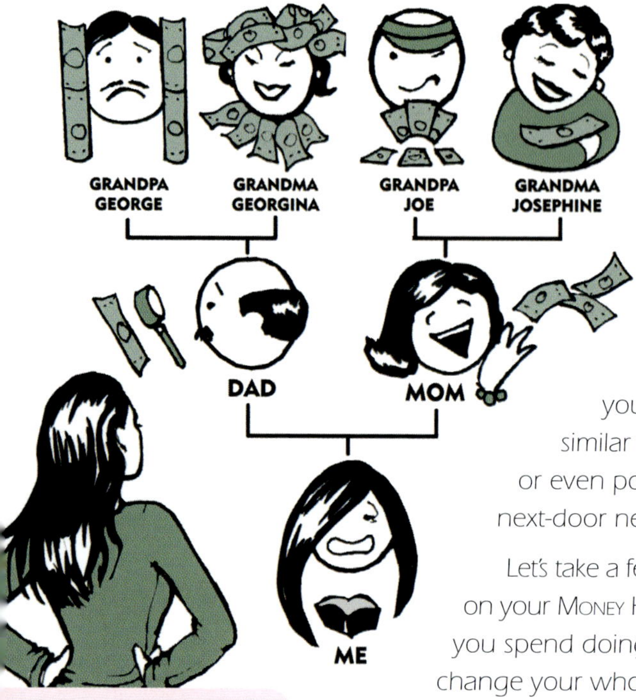

GRANDPA
GEORGE

GRANDMA
GEORGINA

GRANDPA
JOE

GRANDMA
JOSEPHINE

DAD

MOM

ME

Money Heritage Tree™

habits with money. You may find that you have similarities to these people. Maybe you are DATING YOUR MONEY™ like Mom or Dad? You may discover that you are in a relationship with your money that is similar to your brother's or even possibly your next-door neighbor's.

Let's take a few minutes to reflect on your MONEY HERITAGE TREE™. The time you spend doing this exercise may change your whole perspective on money for the rest of your life.

To assist you with building your MONEY HERITAGE TREE™, please go online to www.DatingYourMoney.com. There you'll find the DATING YOUR MONEY CREATE A NEW RELATIONSHIP FORM™, a fill-in-the-blank form that records and stores your information.

Complete the diagram with the people in your life with whom you have had dealings with money. Include people whose money habits and behaviors have influenced you. Take a few minutes for reflection, and then complete the exercise.

As you look at the people on your list, you may discover more about the way your mother, brother, sister, or best friend has chosen to date her or his money. While examining this, you may become aware of the money habits you have adopted from those around you. When you take a look at your money relationship, you may even chuckle when you discover whom you are most similar to.

To build a solid foundation for DATING YOUR MONEY™, consider parting with the negative habits you've adopted from the people on your MONEY HERITAGE TREE™. Money habits are automatic responses, and they do not contribute to a positive financial situation. Not to worry: You will become increasingly aware of your money habits, a necessary step for creating a new relationship with money.

These just aren't me anymore.

Think about the following statement as you look at the MONEY HERITAGE TREE™.

While gaining increased awareness of your own feelings about your money, consider the truth in the statement:

The people in your life have taught you everything you know about money.

You may have been taught that "money is evil," or that "money is the spice of life," or that "dating someone with money is ideal." You may have adopted your parents' methods of approaching your money, and then decided to reject their ways. Take stock of the people who have influenced your thoughts about money and the roles they have played in your life. Look closely to see the parallels between your and their relationships with money. You may have learned tips and tools from significant others that you're not aware of and you use them unthinkingly in your financial life. Do they work for you?

Who taught you about money? There is a world of difference between learning about money in a classroom and learning through experience. Dealing with money, like dating, is a participatory activity—so recognize and identify your earliest financial memories and how they have influenced your present relationship to money. This step is critical to your future success: If you are not enjoying your relationship with money, you may want to date your money in a different way.

Here are a few examples of common money relationships people have:

♥ My parents were savers. They grew up as children of the Great Depression and believe it is not appropriate to waste money on frivolous purchases.

♥ My friend spends everything she has. She is always in debt, and she doesn't hold on to a dollar long. Before you know it, her dollar bills have become a pair of the latest Jimmy Choo shoes.

♥ At the register a man pulls out a wad of cash from his pocket and pays. When you ask him why he pays in cash, he responds: "I've been bankrupt twice, and I want to just get on with my life. I pay in cash so I don't have to file for bankruptcy again."

Observing styles of money management helps you to determine not only what you want in your relationship with money but also what you don't want.

When you want to build a unique relationship with a person or with your money, you need to define what it is that you enjoy and visualize the experience.

You have to let go of experiences that have had a negative impact on your financial relationships so that you can make room for surprising epiphanies.

LET IT GO!

The process of letting go allows psychic space for new realities. In the cash domain, this means you will want to give up Mom and Dad's way of dealing with money or such belief systems as "cash is king." Letting go happens when you, say, clean your closets. As clothes wear out or no longer fit, or you no longer enjoy certain articles of clothing, you give them away. Likewise with your money relationships: You want to leave behind what is not working for you and get ready to create the relationship you desire.

DEFINE IT

Define the relationship that you wish to have with your money and set up your foundation for DATING YOUR MONEY™. Recognize that as your money relationship changes from year to year, you need to keep your DATING YOUR MONEY™ relationship fresh and fun!

In the following exercise you have multiple opportunities to let go of all the unconstructive patterns that have held you back from growing with your money: You get to redefine your present and future relationship to money.

Take a deep breath…now exhale…

On your DATING YOUR MONEY CREATE A NEW RELATIONSHIP FORM™, take a few minutes to answer the questions:

1. What do I want my money to do for me?

2. How do I want to feel about my money?

The following are some sample responses:

I want my money to support my lifestyle.

I want my relationship to money to be easy.

I want my money to be organized and easy to find.

I want my money to make money.

I want to feel good about money.

I want to feel that my money is productive and supportive.

I want to feel that my money is making a positive contribution in the world.

Which responses are closest to your belief system and ideal for building a positive money relationship?

Come back to this step and ask yourself these questions every year to keep your DATING YOUR MONEY™ relationship alive.

YOUR RELATIONSHIP TO MONEY

Defining what you want to experience with your money and how you want to feel about it before building a relationship is critical to your long-term success in DATING YOUR MONEY™.

Rejecting unsupportive modes of behavior and avoiding unhealthy feelings in your financial life are essential. The secret ingredient to creating a long-lasting, healthy relationship with your money is letting go of outdated information and embracing new emotional data to give you a fresh start. In other words, give yourself permission to let go of all the mistakes and misunderstandings you ever had with your money. Replace unpleasant past financial experiences with a shiny new attitude about your budding energetic relationship to money.

When you get involved in a dynamic relationship with your money, you build the life that you desire. You no longer simply accept what comes your way while wondering: "How the heck did I get to this place in my life?"

Using the full arsenal of tools in step one, you will begin experiencing your money (and life!) as exciting and fun.

Go to www.DatingYourMoney.com and celebrate your progress: You're one step closer to fulfilling your dream money relationship.

CONGRATULATIONS!

Chapter 2

Looking for a commitment...

Looking for a long-lasting relationship

Looking for a commitment

Looking for a supportive relationship

Looking for a good communicator

Looking for someone easy to spot in a crowd.

Looking for someone who knows what they want from life and is willing to do whatever it takes to get it.

Looking for someone to grow with

I need a vacation

Looking for a good communicator

Looking for someone easy to spot in a crowd

Looking for someone who knows what they want from

Looking for a commitment

Looking for a supportive relationship

Looking for a good communicator

Looking for someone easy to spot in a crowd

I need a vacation!

Looking for someone to grow with

Looking for a commitment

Looking for a supportive relationship

Looking for a good communicator

Looking for someone easy to spot in a crowd

Looking for someone who knows what they want from life and is willing to do whatever it takes to get it

Looking for someone to

Looking for someone who knows what they want from life and is willing to do whatever it takes to get it.

Looking for someone to grow with

Looking for a long-lasting relationship

Looking for a commitment

Looking for a supportive relationship

Looking for a good communicator

Looking for someone easy to spot in a crowd

I need a vacation...

Looking for someone to grow with

Looking for a

Looking for someone to grow with

Looking for a commitment

Looking for a supportive relationship

Looking for a good communicator

Looking for someone easy to spot in a crowd.

Looking for someone who knows what they want from life and is willing to do whatever it takes to get it.

Looking for a long-lasting relationship

Looking for a commitment

Looking for a supportive relationship

Embracing Change

Looking for a long-lasting relationship

Looking for a commitment

Looking for a supportive relationship

Looking for a good communicator

Looking for someone easy to spot in a crowd.

Looking for someone who knows what they want from

Looking for a long-lasting relationship

Looking for a commitment

Looking for a supportive relationship

Looking for

Looking for a long-lasting relationship

Looking for a commitment

Looking for a supportive relationship

Looking for a good communicator

Looking for someone easy to spot in a crowd.

Looking for someone who knows what they want from life and is willing to do whatever it takes to get it

Looking for someone to grow with

Looking for a long-lasting relationship

Looking for a commitment

Looking for a supportive relationship

I need a vacation ...

Looking for someone easy to spot in

"He just sent me a dozen roses, Mom.
Do you think he's serious?
I'm looking for a commitment!"

Making a Commitment

As you embark upon building a successful relationship with your money, you recognize that something inside you has changed. You have chosen to evolve. **Now you face a new challenge: Focus on your financial aspirations.**

To reach your goals you need to move beyond your emotions of fear, anxiety, joy, exhilaration, and ambivalence. Do you have the resolve to work toward your success? When you reach pivotal moments, do you allow your emotions to distract you from realizing your goals? Have you ever decided to stay the course and make a real commitment to yourself?

In Chapter 2 of DATING YOUR MONEY™, you learn how to make a commitment to yourself, become aware of your emotions and honor them, and move from stating a commitment to making a real commitment so that you get what you want.

STATING A COMMITMENT

Your commitment to yourself and your money begins with a statement of a goal. Stating and making a commitment are very significant decisions in step two of DATING YOUR MONEY™. When the desire to change your life becomes important enough, you will visualize and verbalize what you truly seek in a relationship with your money. There comes a time when your heart aligns with your intentions, making it possible to manifest whatever is important to you. Are you ready to reach your stated goals?

We have the power, which comes from within, to realize whatever we want in our lives—good health, a happy family, satisfying work, fulfilling our religious or spiritual beliefs, and enjoying our money.

By stating a commitment in DATING YOUR MONEY™, you identify with a specific change that you want to make in your life about, for example, how to spend your time, energy, effort, and money to reach a goal.

Examples of making changes in our daily lives include: commitments to eating a more healthy diet, going to the gym to workout, attending our children's activities, spending quality time with our families and friends, delivering our best work, participating in the religious community we belong to, and supporting charitable causes. These are some of the common commitments we make.

I make choices that are consistent with my goals.

When we want to feel healthier, we commit to working out and eating organic foods. We attend a weekly yoga or Pilates class or work out with a personal trainer. When we want to help a charitable or religious organization, we contribute time and money to support efforts in the community. When we feel distant from family members and want to feel closer to them, we commit, say, to calling our mothers twice a week. Equally important is setting aside a date night to spend with a significant other. Likewise, putting our children's ball games, piano lessons, or gymnastics classes on our calendar so that we are there with them is another example of the many commitments we state and keep.

You want to make the same commitment to your relationship with money. When you reach a point where you feel that improving the relationship is a priority, you do whatever it takes to achieve your financial goals.

 Remember: Making a commitment means that we dedicate time, energy, and effort and use every means possible to fulfill our promises to ourselves. Because we are only human, our commitment, dedication, and the pledges we make to ourselves and our money have the potential to be interrupted by…our emotions.

EMOTIONS IN MOTION

Emotions fill our lives. They are at the core of our being—and sometimes they show up when we least expect them.

Ecstasy, triumph, elation, joy, happiness, pleasure, satisfaction, purpose, determination, anxiety, loneliness, sadness, gloom, discouragement, desperation, and misery are all feelings in the spectrum of the human experience.

Now, the task: Consider where your emotions come from so that you can make more informed and better choices in your life. Reflect on the following: How do your emotions respond to information you believe to be accurate? Do your decisions become clouded by your emotions?

When a person smiles at a baby and the infant smiles back, this doesn't necessarily mean that the person who is smiling at the baby delights her. It could be that the baby pooped in her diaper and it feels good! Another example is when a person receives news that someone she cares about has been injured. The emotional response is to become concerned and feel upset or worried. But the friend in question may not be suffering, as the injury was minor and not particularly troublesome.

We smile, laugh, cheer, cry, or frown as a response to our perceptions. Sometimes our feelings have a way of taking over our whole being, too. A person's entire state of being may be altered in response to how she is feeling. Emotions may pass quickly, or they may linger. Have you ever experienced a physical reaction to emotions?

Interesting to note: What's going on inside of you is visible to the outside…

Emotions may surface suddenly when prompted by a specific event or situation. You may be in a conversation with someone when suddenly you feel a rush of frustration. Is it something the person said? Is it something you said or didn't say in the conversation? Either way, you are stuck with an uneasy feeling—and you may not know what caused it. All you know is that the uncomfortable feeling you have is growing.

Our emotional responses to money are equally conflicted. The subject of money is charged with emotions. Becoming aware of your emotions and what you are feeling each time you engage with your finances is important in making a commitment to your money.

Please take a few moments to answer the following questions:

When you are buying a gift for someone, do you feel excited that you have found the perfect gift and you have the money available to purchase it? Do you get a sudden urge to keep the present for yourself?

In general when you write a check, are you delighted or angry? When you pay your bills, do you feel frustrated that you can't balance your checkbook at the end of the month? Do you become discouraged when you are asked for money at bad times of the month? When are those inopportune moments during the month or year when your money is scarce? When you receive money for work you have provided, are you happy or are you upset?

When you take a vacation, do you reserve your room and airline travel in advance so that you focus on the adventure, say, of going to the beach instead of the logistics of planning a trip at the last minute?

When you are buying food and groceries for your home, do you feel fortunate, blessed, worried, or concerned?

In the past, perhaps you may have not given so much thought to the effect of your emotions on your finances. Each time you think about or have an insight into your money, take a moment to check in with yourself to see how you are feeling.

Since emotions come and go quickly, you may want to note them as quickly as possible. The MONEY MOOD METER™ is exactly for this purpose. It is a tool to help you become aware of your feelings about your money!

THE MONEY MOOD METER™

The MONEY MOOD METER™ helps you become aware of what you are feeling when the issue of your money comes up. It is a barometer for assessing your feelings—so that you can gauge your emotional temperature.

For an example of how to best use the MONEY MOOD METER™, go to www.DatingYourMoney.com, and look for the MONEY MOOD METER™ form. It is user-friendly and guides you in exploring your emotions around money.

The MONEY MOOD METER™ is the size of a dollar bill—small enough to carry in your wallet or use as a bookmark. Placing the MONEY MOOD METER™ in strategic places where you interact with money makes the practice of identifying your emotions rapid and effortless. Using it gives you an opportunity to pause during a financial transaction: "How do I feel about my money right now?" It takes the guesswork out of self-discovery: The MONEY MOOD METER™ makes it easy to identify what you're feeling in the moment while connecting with your money.

Here are some suggestions on where to place the MONEY MOOD METER™:

♥ In your wallet alongside your cash and next to your credit cards so that you may examine how you feel before making purchases.

♥ Inside your checkbook to bookmark your next check so you may think about how you feel before writing checks.

♥ On top of your pile of monthly bills so that you may contemplate how you feel before paying them.

THE MONEY MOOD METER™

Ecstatic
Elated
Prosperous

Delighted
Blessed
Joyful

Cheerful
Happy
Pleased

Encouraged
Purposeful
Determined

Anxious
Confused
Concerned

Worried
Disturbed
Depressed

Disappointed
Disillusioned
Defeated

Frustrated
Upset
Angry

💙 On top of your stacks of investment statements so that you may be reminded of your investment strategies.

💙 Next to your computer so you may identify how you feel before making your next online purchase.

The MONEY MOOD METER™ clarifies your emotions so that you know what you are feeling about your finances: The best money decisions are made based on awareness of your feelings and emotions as well as on the hard facts.

A REAL COMMITMENT

Stating a commitment and making a commitment are different. It's very easy to say that you want a healthy relationship with the money in your life. When you are willing to do what it takes and make a commitment to your money, your money relationship will evolve.

❤ **The choices you make regarding what you do about your money—i.e., how you spend your time, energy, and effort on your relationship with money—depend upon your commitment.** To make effective choices, you must remain aware of your emotions. When your feelings in a situation with money do not support a given decision, you may need to question your emotions: Are they working for or against your relationship with money?

Let's look at a sample situation: Judy, a teacher, has made a commitment to herself and her finances and has decided to balance her checkbook. She is not fond of math and has dreaded spending time on the task. Judy soon recognizes, however, that when she keeps her financial information organized and up-to-date, she feels more secure knowing exactly what she has in her account. So what's her goal? It is to stay in touch with her money.

The day after stating her commitment to keep a balanced checkbook, the teacher receives her monthly bank statement. Judy knows that her checkbook is several weeks behind the information in her statement. She is unsure of some of the check numbers and the corresponding sums for the transactions. Remembering the commitment she made to herself, Judy takes out her checkbook and begins to cross-check the statement. She pulls out her MONEY MOOD METER™, which aids her in measuring her feelings: How exactly is she feeling? She recognizes that she is frustrated, anxious, and discouraged.

This is Judy's moment of decision—does she stay true to her commitment and balance that checkbook or give into her emotions, which have convinced her that balancing a checkbook is a formidable task that takes too much time? Will Judy lose sight of her goal and convince herself that she has more important things to do than knowing what she has in her account?

Let's look at another example. Sally, a freelance editor, decides to pay for her food and groceries on a particular credit card to make it easy to track the expense and also to receive points toward an airline ticket for her next trip. She is excited about her statement of commitment to maximize her finances, and she feels good about moving forward. Sally knows that she needs to pay her credit card bill on time so that the costs for the food and groceries are the same as if she paid with cash.

In the supermarket she walks up to the cash register to pay for the items with her credit card. She tries an experiment: Sally pulls out her Money Mood Meter™ and it indicates that she is both excited and worried.

The freelance editor too has reached her moment of decision—will she go through paying with her credit card, making it easier to track the purchase while getting airline points? Is she supporting her commitment to pay her bill on time so that she does not have to spend extra money on interest charges on the credit card purchase? Will her anxiety get the better of her? She questions the worth of paying for it now versus paying later and possibly being penalized for paying late.

In both examples the women either choose to make a commitment to their money or they get lost in their emotions, which ultimately prevents them from making their commitment real.

Emotional responses to financial situations can be put into formulas:

When "E" (your emotions) supports "C" (your commitment), you find it easy to take action and reach your goals:

$$C/E = GOAL$$

Achieving your goal feels effortless when the formula looks like this:

$$C + E = GOAL$$

When "CH" (the choice of actions) brings up "E" (emotions) that are not supportive, your chances of making a real commitment are compromised. Your emotions divide your focus and lead you astray. The following equation illustrates goals that are more difficult to attain:

$$CH/\mathbf{E} = GOAL$$

When your emotions are disproportionate in the equation, you have a more challenging circumstance. So when you commit to a relationship with your money, you always need to ask: Are my decision-making abilities being affected by unsupportive emotions?

YOUR RELATIONSHIP WITH MONEY

It is easy to commit to your relationship with money when you state clearly your commitment and remain aware of your emotions. When you remove yourself from your emotions, you give your relationship with money the undivided attention, time, and effort it deserves. These investments are important and necessary for the steps and activities in DATING YOUR MONEY™.

Now that you have acknowledged your feelings about your money and determined your commitment level, the most effective way to reach your goal of having a truly successful money relationship is:

C/E = Relationship with Money

(Commitment, "C", triumphs over Emotions, "E", so that you may continually build your relationship with your money and become a MONEY DATING ARCHITECT™.)

Remember: You and your money will evolve naturally when you make a commitment to act on behalf of your personal and financial growth!

 To complete the second step in DATING YOUR MONEY™, go to www.DatingYourMoney.com. Celebrate your progress because you're moving fast on developing your ideal money relationship. Today is going to be different because you are closer to reaching your goals.

YOU'RE AWESOME!

"Hey Mom, guess what?!
He's the one!"

Chapter 3

Looking for a supportive relationship…

Looking for a long-lasting relationship
Looking for a commitment
Looking for a supportive relationship
Looking for a good communicator
Looking for someone easy to spot in a crowd.
Looking for someone who knows what they want from life and is willing to do whatever it takes to get it.
Looking for someone to grow with
I need a vacation…
Looking for a good communicator
Looking for someone easy to spot in a crowd.
Looking for someone who knows what they want from

Looking for a commitment
Looking for a supportive relationship
Looking for a good communicator
Looking for someone easy to spot in a crowd
I need a vacation!
Looking for someone to grow with
Looking for a commitment
Looking for a supportive relationship
Looking for a good communicator
Looking for someone easy to spot in a crowd
Looking for someone who knows what they want from life and is willing to do whatever it takes to get it
Looking for someone to

knows what they want from life and is willing to do whatever it takes to get it.
Looking for someone to grow with
Looking for a long-lasting relationship
Looking for a commitment
Looking for a supportive relationship
Looking for a good communicator
Looking for someone easy to spot in a crowd.
I need a vacation…
Looking for someone to grow with
Looking for a

grow with
Looking for a commitment
Looking for a supportive relationship
Looking for a good communicator
Looking for someone easy to spot in a crowd.
Looking for someone who knows what they want from life and is willing to do whatever it takes to get it.
Looking for a long-lasting relationship
Looking for a commitment
Looking for a supportive relationship

who
willing
get it.

Looking for a long-lasting relationship
Looking for a commitment
Looking for a supportive relationship
Looking for a good communicator
Looking for someone easy to spot in a crowd.
Looking for someone who knows what they want from
Looking for a long-lasting relationship
Looking for a commitment
Looking for a supportive relationship
Looking for a commitment
Looking for a supportive relationship
Looking for

Looking for a long-lasting relationship
Looking for a commitment
Looking for a supportive relationship
Looking for a good communicator
Looking for someone easy to spot in a crowd.
Looking for someone who knows what they want from life and is willing to do whatever it takes to get it
Looking for someone to grow with
Looking for a long-lasting relationship
Looking for a commitment
Looking for a supportive relationship
I need a vacation…
Looking for someone easy to spot in

I start relationships and end up feeling alone.

Keeping a Commitment

Armed with knowledge about what you want in a relationship with money, you are ready to seize the day. Confidence and energy surge through your body as you fully commit to your goals. Take a deep breath…

Feeling like you are on an adventure with your finances, you are thrilled as you set out to explore. You are ready to keep your commitment to your money.

As you trace the various financial choices and decisions you make during the day, you are clear-minded about your money relationship. Don't let others derail you and take you away from your goals. When your actions are right on course, you will feel that you've made an excellent money decision. In some areas of your money you'll feel that you have lost your way. Not to worry. You have multiple chances to keep yourself on track. Trust your intuition.

Along the journey, what do you do when your efforts don't produce good results? Do you ask: "What am I doing wrong? Why don't I get results?" Do you feel that you ought to use your efforts and energy toward something more productive than organizing your financial life?

A key moment in the third step of DATING YOUR MONEY™ is when you decide either to continue putting your efforts into growing your money relationship or get out of the game. In some cases, people never return to the game. Don't give up!

Stick with the choices you have made and you'll learn to keep a commitment in your money relationship. Ask yourself:

- ❤ Do I trust myself with my money?

- ❤ Do I know when a money decision works for me and when it doesn't?

💜 Do I know how to use financial information I have picked up to make my next decision?

By asking and answering the hard questions about your finances, you'll maintain your commitment to your relationship with money.

Money Choices

Every day people make decisions about how to use their money for what they want in life. Throughout decision-making, people have days when they feel every choice they make is the right one and that their financial life is running smoothly. On other days they find themselves asking: "How the heck did I ever get to this point with my money?"

Have you ever found yourself in a financial situation that you didn't expect to be in? After making a large purchase, for example, did you ever become cash poor? Did you ever pull out your credit card at the supermarket only to find that it was declined?

When you make a commitment to your relationship with money, you find fewer financial surprises because you decide what your money is doing for you. Being familiar with your money, you make choices so your money works for you.

For example Jane, a physical therapist, has committed to her health and wellness by paying a monthly

"This is not working for me. Something's got to give!"

membership fee to join a gym and exercise regularly. She has decided to spend her money to support her desire for good health. Her decision to join the gym means that she has agreed to pay the monthly membership fee on time. The gym may ask for a credit card for automatic debit payments. Jane will need to check in with her money to make sure she has the amount available each month to pay her credit card bill. Jane wants to make a clear decision about allocating her resources to pay for the gym membership.

Let's examine Jane's situation. (1) Jane is committed to better health, fitness, and wellness. To fulfill her commitment, she contemplates joining a gym. She wants her money to support her priorities. (2) Jane determines that she has the resources to pay the monthly membership fee. (3) She pays by credit card and the gym bills her monthly. (4) She knows that she needs to set aside the membership fee each month in order to pay the amount in full. (5) She has made a conscious financial decision to spend her money on exercise so that she reaps the benefits of good health.

Consciously or unconsciously you make decisions every day about your money. How you choose to position yourself with a little help from your money determines whether your finances support your goals or not.

Is your money helping you reach your goals?

After making decisions about how to distribute your cash, you'll want to check in often with your money to gauge your commitment to each other: Is your money helping you reach your goals or is it taking you away from what you want?

WHEN MONEY IS WORKING FOR YOU

In keeping a commitment to your relationship with money, be aware of the financial choices you make. After making a choice about how best to allocate your monies, check in with yourself and ask the following questions. Pay close attention your responses.

1. "Why am I choosing to spend/save/donate/invest my money now?"

2. "What do I expect to accomplish as a result of my financial choices?"

3. "What do I want my money to do for me and my life?"

Your answers to the questions increase your awareness of daily choices you make about money. Becoming aware of your financial habits is important. Seeing your unique patterns with money helps you to clarify your choices and goals.

Back to Jane, the physical therapist. When she looked at how she positioned herself with her money, she prioritized her health. In joining the gym, she went faithfully each week, felt fabulous, and paid the monthly gym membership on her credit card bill promptly.

Jane's choices were consistent with her commitments to herself. Her spending decisions supported her commitments to herself and her money because she loved what she was doing with her income.

When your life is rich—full and comfortable—chances are the choices you'll make for yourself and your money are right.

WHEN MONEY ISN'T WORKING FOR YOU

When you are confused about your money, i.e., wonder where your money goes and why your finances never add up at the end of each month, it is time to look closely at your relationship with money to see which areas in your financial life need fixing. In other words, if your money is not doing what you want it to do, you need to take a few moments to identify and review the choices you have made and why they don't work for you. The financial decisions you make today ultimately determine whether your money will be there to support you in the future.

Let's return to our friend Jane and her success at the gym. What if Jane decides not to pay the balance in full on her credit card for the monthly gym membership? When she originally signed up for the gym, the commitment she made to herself was to pay her membership fee in full each month when she received her bill. If Jane decides to pay the minimum balance on her credit card bill, she is now making a different choice with her money, which is not consistent with the commitment she promised to keep.

If Jane continues the same spending habit of not paying the credit card balance for the gym membership, she will find that the cost of the membership fee is higher because of the interest she incurs. So she is spending more than she originally committed for her health and wellness program. This course of action is not only out of sync with her commitment to her money but also makes her feel concerned about breaking her promises.

In an extreme situation, say, by not paying the balance in full after several months, Jane maxes out her credit. The card company then rejects payments to the gym. The gym decides not to allow Jane access to the facilities because her credit card has been declined. Now Jane is stuck in an unsupportive relationship with her money, and she is upset and disappointed.

Understanding the choices you make that don't get you what you want is as important as recognizing the decisions that have gotten you excellent results. In fact, you may learn more about yourself from your mistakes because you truly comprehend what you need to change in your relationship with money.

CELEBRATING CHOICES—WHETHER OR NOT YOUR MONEY IS WORKING FOR YOU

When you are committed to making your money relationship work, you feel fulfilled. Your financial decisions are consistent with what you want in your life—and you and your money are positioned to support one another.

When you experience problems in the relationship, look at the choices you've made and don't be afraid to explore why your choices aren't working. For example, examining what has gone wrong with your cash flow provides valuable insight: You'll learn not to repeat patterns that don't produce the results you desire.

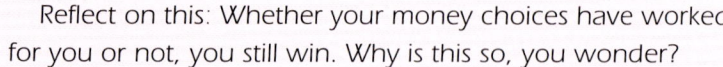 Reflect on this: Whether your money choices have worked for you or not, you still win. Why is this so, you wonder?

When the financial choices you've made are working in your relationship with money, celebrate the joy and ease of your life. When you discover what isn't productive in your relationship with money, celebrate what you are learning about making new choices. Celebrating the choices you make at every stage of your financial life, you are deepening your commitment to your relationship with money and growing all the while.

GROWING WITH YOUR MONEY

You are constantly growing and changing every day. You gather information and discover new interests as you let go of the incidents in your life that no longer have meaning. You may find that the choices you have made for you and your money work for a time. A few weeks or months later, your financial planning no longer seems to be working because you have changed. Your priorities are different, but your money situation is still the same. Does this sound like you?

Try this: Take eight minutes each month to check in with yourself... Are the choices I am making for myself and my money consistent with what I want in my life today?

Recognizing the need to change your choices and decisions about your money is the secret to your overall success in keeping your commitment alive and enjoyable in your relationship with money. Keeping the commitment fresh is essential for a healthy money relationship.

Now, take the time to think about your financial preferences. How do you stay on track with your resolutions? Close your eyes and visualize the answer. It'll be different for everybody. Think about enjoying your money at every stage in the process of growing with your finances. Do you love what your money does for you every day? Honor the thought either way.

When you keep the commitment to DATING YOUR MONEY™, you begin to experience your money (and your life!) as delightful and satisfying. Yes–you are well on your way to becoming a MONEY DATING ARCHITECT™.

Go to www.DatingYourMoney.com. Throw a party and dance the night away because you're one step closer to keeping your commitment to your dream money relationship!

EXCELLENT TANGO!

Chapter 4

Looking for a good communicator...

Looking for a long-lasting relationship
Looking for a commitment
Looking for a supportive relationship
Looking for a good communicator
Looking for someone easy to spot in a crowd
Looking for someone who knows what they want from life and is willing to do whatever it takes to get it
Looking for someone to grow with
I need a vacation...
Looking for a good communicator
Looking for someone easy to spot in a crowd
Looking for someone who knows what they want from

Looking for a commitment
Looking for a supportive relationship
looking for a good communicator
Looking for someone easy to spot in a crowd
I need a vacation!
Looking for someone to grow with
Looking for a commitment
Looking for a supportive relationship
Looking for a good communicator
Looking for someone easy to spot in a crowd
Looking for someone who knows what they want from life and is willing to do whatever it takes to get it.
Looking for someone to grow with
Looking for a

they want from life and is willing to do whatever it takes to get it.
Looking for someone to grow with
Looking for a long-lasting relationship
Looking for a commitment
Looking for a supportive relationship
Looking for a good communicator
Looking for someone easy to spot in a crowd.
Looking for someone who knows what they want from life and is willing to do whatever it takes to get it.
Looking for a long-lasting relationship
Looking for a commitment
Looking for a supportive relationship

grow with
Looking for a commitment
Looking for a supportive relationship
Looking for a good communicator
Looking for someone easy to spot in a crowd
Looking for someone who knows what they want from life and is willing to do whatever it takes to get it
Looking for a long-lasting relationship
Looking for a commitment
Looking for a supportive relationship
Looking for

Looking for a long-lasting relationship
Looking for a commitment
Looking for a supportive relationship
Looking for a good communicator
Looking for someone easy to spot in a crowd.
Looking for someone who knows what they want from life and is willing to do whatever it takes to get it
Looking for someone to grow with
Looking for a long-lasting relationship
Looking for a commitment
Looking for a supportive relationship
I need a vacation...
Looking for someone easy to spot in

He never calls anymore...

Communicating and Connecting with Your Money

As you turn your thoughts to your money today, you realize that you don't really know where to begin. Do you feel all psyched up about organizing your finances and then suddenly get intimidated about moving forward with such an overwhelming undertaking?

No matter! You are committed already to the relationship—and now you need only to track down your monies to start building your dreams. A relationship connects seemingly disparate people and things—so in order for you to build your relationship with your money, you have to go to the source. Connect with your cash for a moment and answer these questions:

- ♥ How do I relate to the money in my life?
- ♥ Do I know how and where to get essential information on my finances?

In the fourth step of DATING YOUR MONEY™ you learn how to make your money accessible so it is easy for you to relate to. When you bring up the subject of money, you need to be aware of the language you use when speaking about it—and how others talk about it with you. Devoting time and attention is essential in communicating and connecting with money so that you both grow and prosper.

THE MONEY CONNECTION

Communication is the heart of every relationship. The more you know about your money, the more it grows. The better informed you are about your finances, the faster you grow.

To connect with your money, begin by working on yourself. What is the easiest method for you to receive and understand information? Perhaps you like to surf the Internet, fill out electronic forms, and communicate by e-mail? Do you prefer receiving hard-copy documents and forms on which you check, circle, and highlight important information about your money? Maybe you like obtaining information from automated information lines or speaking with representatives who assist you by phone. Another shortcut to gathering information is working with a consultant or specialist who assists you in your money relationship—working together you get the information you seek and need.

The secret to unlocking your Money Connection is: Know your style of communication and stay true to it. This means you get information your way.

Reflect on... When you do research on a subject, including studying your money, do you follow your instincts to find information quickly and effectively?

The following are some of the methods people use for gathering information. Which do you use?

- ♥ You send e-mail to friends, colleagues, or business associates.

- ♥ You surf the Internet and type in keywords in a search engine like Google or Yahoo!

- ♥ You write a letter to a person or company requesting information.

- ♥ You dial a company number and listen to automated information.

- You bypass the company menu and speak with a customer representative to make a direct inquiry.

- You ask an expert for a few minutes of her time to share her experience, insight, and knowledge about a particular area.

- You set up a lunch date with an expert on a subject you are interested in.

- You hire a consultant for information.

Identifying your primary mode of getting information, following your methods of inquiry, and being consistent when connecting with your money add to the foundation in building your relationship to money.

THE LANGUAGE OF MONEY

Connections are made when we exchange information with another person. For example when we want to make a purchase, we ask a salesperson for the price. We receive a clear answer—the cost of the item. The exchange of information is communicated in a few words. A salesperson rings up the item and you hand over the twenty dollars. The exchange is straightforward.

Easy-to-understand language is best for a simple exchange of information. Explore the language of money that is easiest for you to understand. Seek information about your money in a language that is most comfortable for you. When you accomplish this task in step four, your money becomes effortless to connect with.

For example, Susan is a musician who plays in a band. Her understanding of money is: "When I play, I get paid. When I sell a CD, I get paid." This is her reference to money, and she tunes out when someone talks about creating other income streams that do not require her to contribute as much time, energy, or effort. There is nothing wrong with Susan—she is simply unfamiliar with investment language. Susan decides to be proactive. She has an acquaintance in finance and asks him to explain investing in terms that make sense to a musician. Finance now rocks with her, and when her buddy brings up finances—Susan gets it.

When you work on your relationship to money, seek information in a financial language that is easy to understand. When you find information about your money is not being presented to you in language you can follow, look to other people and places for communication. Confide in people—let them know the level of your understanding of money talk. Explain that you want to learn more about your relationship with money. Let people help and give you financial information: You will develop beautiful relationships with all sorts of folks, and your money will grow and prosper. You begin to understand your money better while connecting to people involved in the process of building your finances.

CAN WE TALK?

Your money is available to you for making positive connections in the world. The adage "Timing is everything" applies to your relationship with your money. The more time you spend with your money, the more your relationship will grow.

There is a misconception that you have to spend a lot of time with your money. The truth is you need to spend quality time with your money to build a relationship. Investing quality time means that you understand your MONEY CONNECTION STYLE™ and use a money language that you can rely on. **Consistently spending quality time with your finances is key to building your relationship with money. Without spending quality time in the relationship, you will drift apart and your money will feel like a burden.**

To enjoy the experience of growing your money relationship, you want to set aside quality time to spend with your money. Create a specific time and space where you have access to information and use a language to deepen your money connection. For example, Jessica has a date with her money every Sunday evening from 7:30 to 8. Her MONEY CONNECTION STYLE™ is both electronic and digital—she meets her money on her computer at her desk at home. She surfs the net for information and has a Money Connection folder on her desktop in which she saves whatever she finds interesting in the money language that she is comfortable with. Her relationship with money has become effortless and fun.

By consistently spending quality time with her money, Jessica has gathered valuable information to make better choices about her money and what she wants in her life. She is actively building a long-lasting relationship with money that will grow and prosper. Each week, you'll need to talk with your money too!

"Call me."

CONNECTING WITH YOUR MONEY

Now that you know and practice your MONEY CONNECTION STYLE™, have a time and place where you meet up with your money. **Matching your MONEY CONNECTION STYLE™ to your money language is a recipe for success in DATING YOUR MONEY™.**

Take a look at an example of putting the money relationship puzzle pieces together. Jill does her banking online. Her brokerage account statements are also available online. In addition, Jill uses a software package for tracking her expenses. Her MONEY CONNECTION STYLE™ is electronic. Jill is also a personal trainer, so let's put her money into terms she can relate to.

She does a Money Connection warm-up by researching information about her money electronically before dating her money. She takes several deep breaths, relaxes her mind, body, and spirit, and is now prepared to spend quality time with her cash.

She digs in: It is easy for her to refer to the places where her money is saved and invested; when and from whom she receives money; how many times a week/month/year she receives income; and her spending habits.

The process of checking in electronically with her finances takes less than thirty minutes at a time because she has set up an efficient Money Connection. She understands her financial picture online, and based on it she makes informed decisions that feel clear and comfortable to her.

A few hints to integrate your money language into your Money Connection:

💜 If your Money Connection is made electronically, contact your banking institution, your brokerage and/or investment companies, your credit card companies, and others to whom you pay monthly bills for online access to your accounts. Register for online bill payments and schedule them for all monthly bills. Set up direct deposit for consistent income streams. Use a software program to track and review your expenses. Organizing your finances online provides you fast and easy access to information about your money during the quality time you spend DATING YOUR MONEY™.

💜 If you connect to your money by looking at hard copies of statements and accounts, contact your bank, your brokerage or investment companies, your credit card companies, and those to whom you pay monthly bills, and find out the exact dates when statements are mailed to you. Ask the service representatives at the various places you conduct business with when your billing cycles begin and end—and if you wish, change the dates of your billing cycles to coordinate the time when your income is deposited in your account with the dates you pay your expenses. In a notebook or journal, track and write down your monthly spending and earnings. Tracking the flow of your earnings and payments and paying attention to your statements afford you quality time with your money.

💜 If you connect to your money in person exclusively, contact the financial institutions with which you do business and set up quarterly appointments to review your accounts. Keep your appointments and be on time. Check with your bookkeeper and accountant to see whether their records are accurate. Learn to assist the people you have hired to manage your money so that you are spending quality time with your money and maximizing opportunities for you and your money.

The faster you plug in to the flow of information about your money, the easier it becomes to spend quality time and have a long-lasting relationship with it.

The DATING YOUR MONEY™ relationship begins and ends with communication. To grow and prosper as a MONEY DATING ARCHITECT™: (**1**) Identify your MONEY CONNECTION STYLE™. (**2**) Seek and request information in the language you use to understand your money. (**3**) Focus time and energy on building a relationship with your money—so that spending quality time with it feels natural and productive!

Ready—set—go to www.DatingYourMoney.com, and celebrate your progress: You're one step closer to realizing your dream money relationship...

ENJOY—BECAUSE YOU'RE TERRIFIC!

Chapter 5

Looking for someone easy to spot in a crowd…

Looking for a long-lasting relationship

Looking for a commitment

Looking for a supportive relationship

Looking for a good communicator

Looking for someone easy to spot in a crowd

Looking for someone who knows what they want from life and is willing to do whatever it takes to get it

Looking for someone to grow with

I need a vacation…

Looking for a good communicator

Looking for someone easy to spot in a crowd

Looking for someone who knows what they want from

If only my money was more organized,
I would know where it was.

Organizing Your Money

You are accomplishing so much in your relationship with money. You know how to communicate with your cash and make finances easy to understand. Now let's start working with dollars and…sense.

Money is a disorganized affair—it's all over the place, in different accounts at various institutions and maybe stuffed under your mattress at home! Many people cringe when they have to sit down with their money and straighten it out. They feel it will take forever to organize. Do you feel this way too? Perhaps you deal with only one aspect of your money at a time, such as your expenses. You never get a complete picture of the state of your finances because the parts never seem to add up to a whole. Do you believe it will take days to sift through all your financial information? After a few attempts at getting the numbers straight, do you feel frustrated and give up on your money?

In the fifth step of DATING YOUR MONEY™, you learn to track down your money. You see clearly the ebb and flow of your revenue and expenditures. You behold your well-organized financial information and comprehend it quickly and effortlessly, so the quality time you set aside for DATING YOUR MONEY™ is pleasantly spent.

I'm organizing my money so I know when it is coming and going.

GETTING IT STRAIGHT

To assist you with information on cleaning up your act, go to www.DatingYourMoney.com and click on the ORGANIZING YOUR MONEY RAINMAKER WORKBOOK™. You are given space to tidy up your financial information so you continue DATING YOUR MONEY™.

WHERE IT COMES FROM

When you're DATING YOUR MONEY™ and contemplating getting serious, ask yourself: Does money magically appear in my life or is it the result of my hard work? Understand the way money enters your life and how you feel about its daily presence. Do you wish it were here to stay or do you wish it would leave you alone?

The following is a list of sources of income. How much and how often do you receive income from each:

● A paycheck from your company or job

● Accounts such as bank and brokerage that generate interest income

● Investments that produce dividend income

● Real estate investments that provide positive net income and cash flow for you on a monthly basis

● Your own business and its accounts receivable

● Income paid to you from your own business

● Internet marketing business that produces income daily, weekly, monthly, or quarterly

● Affiliate income from referrals to other people's businesses

- 💜 Collectibles that you buy and sell or auction that generate a profit

- 💜 Income resulting from a legal agreement

 Gathering information about your money, you see your financial picture clearly so that you make educated choices about your assets. In the ORGANIZING YOUR MONEY RAINMAKER WORKBOOK™, describe your various income streams and when money is deposited into your accounts. The workbook is available at www.DatingYourMoney.com.

OTHER MONEY SOURCES

In addition to the money we earn, money is available to us from other sources, such as credit cards, credit lines, and loans. Credit is one of the most problematic areas because it is money that you are borrowing now with a promise to pay later. It has the greatest potential to spin out of control. In most cases, loans cost you a lot of money unless you pay them back within a limited timeframe.

As you continue to examine your money and shed light on your financial situation, you will want to organize information about your money in the workbook so that you have easy access to it. By consolidating your credit and loan information, you will see your liabilities clearly and make choices about what you actually owe. Write down in the workbook your responses to the following questions about your credit cards, credit lines, and loans:

- 💜 How many institutions have extended credit to me? List them.

- 💜 Did I ask for specific credit lines or did the companies set the credit limits for me?

- Do I respond to promotional offers for balance transfers?

- What are the amounts of credit I have for each credit card or loan? How many of my credit lines do I use?

- How much credit is currently available to me?

- What are the interest rates on my credit cards, lines of store credit, and loans?

- Do I pay annual fees for any of my credit resources? How much do I pay?

- What are my minimum payments each month? How much do I usually pay toward my balances?

- What benefits do I receive from using credit resources? (Examples of benefits are cash back, airline miles, or reward points you use toward other purchases.)

- Am I using the benefits from my credit resources? Do my benefits expire if I don't use them within a particular time?

- Are there any other fees attached to my credit resources (such as for late payments, etc.)? How often are these fees on my bill?

- How often do I review my credit card statements or lines of credit to confirm their accuracy?

- Do I know how to correct any errors creditors may make and erroneously post to my accounts?

- Do I know the special procedures or instructions for using my credit cards or lines of credit overseas? For accessing cash advances? For making payments?

Please refer to your copy of the **credit questionnaire** in the ORGANIZING YOUR MONEY RAINMAKER WORKBOOK™. Use the form to organize your money. You will be able to review your information on your finances quickly and add to the information each year as you continue DATING YOUR MONEY™.

EASY COME, EASY GO?

Where and how fast your money comes and goes is up to you. Tracking your money shows you the results of your choices and actions. If you don't know where your money is going, how will you know if it is working for you the way you want it to? Note, we are not talking about budgeting money. Instead we are speaking about taking control of your money and positioning it to work for you so you get what you want out of life.

Working together with your money, you want to know what you are doing with it and the results of your actions. Then you can analyze what is working well with your money and where you may want to make some changes.

Go to the ORGANIZING YOUR MONEY RAINMAKER WORKBOOK™ link at www.DatingYourMoney.com. Fill out the DATING YOUR MONEY W2 FORM™, which assists you in organizing your financial information—including the section on where and when you spend your money to support your lifestyle, goals, and dreams.

The following is a list of areas where you may be spending your money. Identify where your cash goes:

Entertainment—Entertainment is when we enjoy our lives doing activities we like with friends and business colleagues.

What types of entertainment do you enjoy? Do you often go to the movies or to the theater? Do you watch cable television? Do you entertain at home? Do you go to other people's homes? How often do you enjoy entertainment activities? What does it cost when you go out or entertain at home?

Gifts—Giving is one of life's greatest experiences. When we give gifts, people are delighted because we have thought of them. Do you like to give gifts to family, friends, colleagues, or friends of your children? When do you give gifts during the year? Is there a time when you give many gifts, for example a month filled with family and friends' birthdays or a month of anniversaries? Maybe many of your friends are getting married or having babies this year.

Charitable Donations—Charity is a gift of the heart to those who are less fortunate and require assistance. It may be economic, physical, medical, or spiritual. Do you give gifts to charity? How do you give these gifts? Do you make gifts of money? Or do you donate other items, like clothes or cars? When do you give gifts? Do you give them throughout the year, or toward one part of the year, such as at the end of the year during the holiday season?

Recreation and Hobbies—Exercising the mind, body, and spirit creates balance and brings joy to our lives. Our special skills and talents manifest themselves when our mind, body, and soul are in harmony. What do you enjoy doing that stimulates your entire being? How do you exercise? Do you go to the gym? Do you do yoga? Are you a cyclist, runner, or hiker? What are your hobbies and interests? Are you a gardener, a quilter, or a car restoration aficionado? Do you read novels? Belong to a book club? How often do you enjoy these activities? What do they cost?

Dues—Some activities we enjoy are done in a group or in an association. Do you belong to organizations? How many do you participate in regularly? How often does each group meet? Do you often go to the meetings or attend group functions? Consider the cost of each group you wish to join, and the return on the investment of your time and money.

Subscriptions—Information is available in so many different forms and methods of delivery. Subscriptions help us keep up with topics that interest us. Do you enjoy receiving and reading daily newspapers, weekly or monthly magazines or newsletters? Do you pay for an Internet service provider? Do you subscribe to online services? How much are you paying to be plugged in technologically?

Travel—Do you love to see and experience the world? Where do you like to travel generally? What kind of trips do you enjoy taking: Do you take long weekends or enjoy going on longer trips of a week or more? Do you enjoy trips to the great outdoors, which involve camping, or do you prefer staying in five-star hotels? Do you drive, fly, or take the train or bus to your travel destinations? What and where do you like to eat when you travel? Do you enjoy traveling alone? Do you enlist the help of travel agents and tour guides? How often do you travel? How much do you typically spend on trips?

W²: The What & When of Your Money

Client: _____

What	Amount	Due How Often?	When You Pay It	Amount You Pay
Entertainment/Gifts/Recreation/Hobbies				
Cable TV				
Internet				

Pets—Pets, like people, incur expenses. Owners pay for their pets because they love them, and life would not be the same without their pets. What are you feeding your beloved pet? Do you buy routine items for your pet's care—like litter box liners, pooper-scoopers, or treats? What about toys and clothes for your pet? How often do you buy these items? How often do you take your pet to the veterinarian? Does your pet have any condition that requires special products, treatments, or activities? Do you train your pet? Do you hire someone to assist you with your pet's care and training? How often do you hire a pet-care specialist and how much do you spend?

Children—Children bring beauty and grace to humanity, and they are expensive too! Parents foot their children's many bills and expenses because they adore their kids and it's their responsibility to support them. How expensive are your kids? Do they go to private school? What activities are your children involved in that cost money? What do they do after school? What activities do they enjoy during the weekends? Do they dance, do karate, swim, or participate in religious school and religious activities? Do they attend summer camp? Do they receive an allowance? Do you have a nanny or baby-sitter? How much do you spend on childcare?

Education—Education is for children and grown-ups. Adults purchase books, pay for classes, workshops, and seminars, and sometimes buy home-study CD programs to increase their understanding and knowledge of a particular subject or skill. How do you further your education? Do you take continuing education classes at a local school or university? Do you attend seminars or special training classes? Do you enjoy home-study courses? Do you take classes offered through your religious organization or other associations you belong to? How do you learn more in your life—and how much does each activity that you engage in cost?

Housing/Property—Owning your own home is the American dream. Whether you own your home or rent from a landlord, shelter is a basic human need that requires money. Do you rent or own your home? How many properties do you own, and what are the annual costs of the homes? Do you have a mortgage? Do you pay real estate taxes, property taxes, or school taxes? How much do you pay for electricity, water, or oil that is provided to your home? Do you have a landscaper or lawn care team? Do you have a snow removal service in the winter? What do you do when your home needs to be repaired? Do you spend money on home improvements?

Transportation and Automobiles—Getting from point A to point B often involves some form of transportation. Do you use public transportation, taxis, or a private car or limousine service? Do you own your own car or do you lease one? How old is your car? How often do you buy fuel for your car? How much gas does the tank hold and how much do you pay at the pump? Do you pay highway tolls in your area? How often do you bring in your car for inspections and maintenance? Does your car require repairs? Do you pay a vehicle tax? How much is your car insurance?

Food—Everybody loves to eat—whether it's a meal made by an executive chef or a peanut butter and jelly sandwich on the go. Do you enjoy eating out? How often do you dine at restaurants in a week? Do you eat out for breakfast, lunch, or dinner? Do you enjoy food shopping? How often do you go to the market? Do you shop at a variety of places? What kinds of foodstuff do you purchase? Do you buy specialty grocery items from out of state? How much do you spend on food per week?

Liquor and Wine—Some people celebrate life with alcohol and wine. What types of alcoholic beverages do you enjoy? Do you purchase a variety of liquors for your home? How often do you stock up? Do you enjoy the taste of fine wines, their vintage, provenance, and bouquet? How often do you purchase wine for your home? Do you visit wineries? Do you seek collectible bottles for your wine cellar? How much do you spend on liquor and wine per week?

Tobacco Products—Others enjoy tobacco products: cigarettes, cigars, and pipe tobacco. Do you use tobacco products? How often do you purchase them? Do you collect cigars and have a humidor?

When my money is organized it's easier to track and I make better choices.

Do you have collectible pipes that you display or share in your home or office? How much do you spend on tobacco products per week?

Clothing—In many societies, clothing is a symbol for an individual's good taste. Shopping for clothing is also a pastime because it provides fun and enjoyment—different styles and colors of clothing brighten our worlds. Where do you buy your clothes? Are the clothing shops close to home? Do you purchase your duds while on vacation? Do you make special trips to outlets or shopping malls? Are you a seasonal shopper, or do you shop for clothing all year round? Do you purchase an article of clothing when it catches your eye? Are you an impulse shopper? Do you change sizes from time to time, requiring that you purchase new clothes or take the ones you have to the tailor? Do you buy clothing for your children? How often do they require new clothes? How much do you spend on clothing each season?

Banks, Credit Lines, and Loans—As mentioned earlier in this chapter, some of your money may cost you money. How much do you incur in bank charges each month? Do you pay checking fees, online banking fees, or ATM fees? Are you assessed fees for overdrafts, bounced checks, late payments, or any other special services? Do you use your credit cards more frequently than cash? What are the APRs on the credit cards? How much of the principal do you pay back monthly on your loans? What kinds of loans do you have: student loans, car loans, personal loans?

Divorce Agreements and Obligations—When our relationships grow apart, our financial arrangements are affected too. Are you divorced or are you in the process of getting divorced? Does your agreement require maintenance payments? How much do you pay or how much do you receive? How many years will you pay or receive maintenance? Does your agreement include child support? What is the amount, and for how long do you pay or receive child support?

Medical and Dental—Our bodies are our temples. We must support our bodies so they support us. How do you take care of yours? Do you have a physical exam each year? Do you have a specialist for any particular conditions? Do you go regularly to the dentist? Do you need any special dental work? Do you wear braces? Do your children wear braces? Do your children see a doctor for any particular conditions? Do they see the doctor several times a year due to colds or other conditions? Do you take prescription medications? How often do you take vitamins or supplements to maintain your health? Do you see a chiropractor, acupuncturist, or other alternative health practitioner? Do you total your medical and dental costs annually and give the information to your accountant to write off (up to the maximum amount allowed) in your tax returns?

Personal Care—To take good care of ourselves we create healthy routines in our lives. What are your personal care and beauty routines? Do you cut, color, straighten, perm, or highlight your hair? How often do you go the hair salon? Do you get your clothes cleaned and pressed? How often do you go to the laundry and dry cleaners? Do you get a monthly manicure and pedicure? Do you enjoy a facial occasionally? Do you ever indulge in getting massages or body treatments? What do you pay annually for your personal care?

Insurance—We often seek to protect what we feel is valuable in our lives. Do you have health and dental insurance? What about life or disability insurance? Have you ever thought about long-term care insurance for yourself or your aging parents? Do you have renters' or homeowners' insurance? What about automobile insurance—and perhaps an umbrella policy? Do you have pet insurance—or another type of insurance? Do you have handy the names for each insurance company that holds your policies, and the costs for each premium payment? When are the payments due and how do you pay—monthly, quarterly, every six months or annually?

Telephone/Communication—We're all connected—and wired—for better or worse. How do you communicate with people in your life? Do you call them on your land-line or cell phone? Do you make many long distance telephone calls, or do you like e-mail? Maybe you prefer snail mail to instant messages? Do you have a pager, a BlackBerry, or another high-tech wireless communication device? What is the total monthly expenditure for your communication needs?

Advisory Team—Many of us build a team of people with special skills to support and guide us in areas in which we lack expertise. Who is on your team? Do you have a team of advisors, such as attorneys, accountants, bank professionals, financial advisors, business partners, or construction specialists? What are their professional fees? How much and how often do you pay them?

Miscellaneous Expenses—Some expenses don't seem to fit into any of the categories mentioned. Some may be deductible and others unreimbursed expenses. Do you have a flexible spending account available through your company? Do you have a health savings account? Do you pre-pay your transportation costs through TransitChek or a similar service? Do you take advantage of special tax filing status programs offered through your employer or the government?

You may have other expenses that are specific to your lifestyle. Do you buy flowers for yourself or others? Do you purchase stamps or use special mailing services? Do you ship gifts express mail at particular times of the year or for special occasions?

Cash–One quick note about cash: When it comes to accounting for what you spend, cash is challenging. While DATING YOUR MONEY™ pay attention to your cash flow by examining the frequency and amounts of your cash withdrawals from your accounts. To get a grip on what you are spending, carry a small notebook or digital device to record your daily cash expenditures.

The key to tracking your cash is to record your spending each day in a ledger, in a spreadsheet (Microsoft Excel), or with the help of a software package like Quicken or Microsoft Money. If you don't transfer the information to one centralized document, you end up with notebooks filled with scribble, out-of-control digital data, or millions of crumpled paper receipts that clutter your space and cloud your judgment about where your cash is actually going.

If you want to know where your cash is going when DATING YOUR MONEY™, track it using the most efficient method for you for a period of at least thirty days—either use the software program mentioned or a notebook. This will show you where you are using (and enjoying) the cash in your life. Include this information in your DATING YOUR MONEY W2 FORM™.

The tracking exercise prepares you to complete the DATING YOUR MONEY W2 FORM™, which provides you with insight and information about your money that you may not be aware of. Imagine how far you can go with your money once you understand your spending habits. **One simple step of organization demonstrates the control you ultimately have over your money.** The DATING YOUR MONEY W2 FORM™ helps you identify where you want to make a change so that you may choose a different way to work with your money so it works for you.

THE BIG PICTURE

Organizing your money allows for mutual growth, while DATING YOUR MONEY™ supports you in owning your relationship with your money. Are you willing to commit to an action plan—to make changes along your journey when you find the choices you have made are not supporting what you want with your money?

Your chances of enjoying a satisfying connection with your money are much greater when you communicate clearly and effectively with your resources. Putting the pieces together at the beginning of the DATING YOUR MONEY™ relationship changes your outlook on your money and your life forever. Often we focus our energy on the end result—in DATING YOUR MONEY™ the journey of continual discovery of your relationship with money is the most powerful experience of all.

As a MONEY DATING ARCHITECT™, you invest time and energy in yourself and your money to get huge returns in the future. Go girl: You're one step closer to DATING YOUR MONEY™ for the rest of your life!

TERRIFIC!

Now that I've organized my money,
I feel confident and self-assured.

Chapter 6 :08

Looking for a long-lasting relationship
Looking for a commitment
Looking for a supportive relationship
Looking for a good communicator
Looking for someone easy to spot in a crowd.
Looking for someone who knows what they want from life and is willing to do whatever it takes to get it.
Looking for someone to grow with
I need a vacation...
Looking for a good communicator
Looking for someone easy to spot in a crowd.
Looking for someone who knows what they want from

Looking for a commitment
Looking for a supportive relationship
Looking for a good communicator
Looking for someone easy to spot in a crowd
I need a vacation...
Looking for someone to grow with
Looking for a commitment
Looking for a supportive relationship
Looking for a good communicator
Looking for someone easy to spot in a crowd
Looking for someone who knows what they want from life and is willing to do whatever it takes to get it.
Looking for someone to

Looking for someone who knows what he wants from life and is willing to do whatever it takes to get it...

a crowd.
Looking for a supportive relationship
Looking for a good communicator
Looking for someone easy to spot in a crowd
I need a vacation...
Looking for someone to grow with
Looking for a

someone easy to spot in a crowd.
Looking for someone who knows what they want from life and is willing to do whatever it takes to get it.
Looking for a long-lasting relationship
Looking for a commitment
Looking for a supportive relationship
Looking for

Looking for a long-lasting relationship
Looking for a commitment
Looking for a supportive relationship
Looking for a good communicator
Looking for someone easy to spot in a crowd.
Looking for someone who knows what they want from life and is willing to do whatever it takes to get it.
Looking for someone to grow with
Looking for a long-lasting relationship
Looking for a commitment
Looking for a supportive relationship
I need a vacation...
Looking for someone easy to spot in

"I want you to work out with me 8 minutes a week."

Dating Your Money™
in 8 Minutes a Week

As you look at the steps you have taken to build your relationship with money, you are prepared to move forward with your commitment to Dating Your Money™.

You have explored your Money Heritage Tree™ and learned what you want to change in your money relationship. You have let go of old ideas that no longer support you; you are not afraid to examine your emotions and use the Money Mood Meter™ to check in with your feelings; and you make sound decisions about your money while honoring how you feel.

After identifying your Money Connection Style™ for winning communication and awesome organizational skills in your financial life, you know everything there is to know about your money: your sources of income, how and when you receive money, and how and when you spend your money. Remember: take time to celebrate what you learn about yourself and your finances, and continue devoting your time, energy and effort to building a solid relationship with your money. You are more than ready to commit to Dating Your Money™.

In the sixth chapter of Dating Your Money™, you learn an easy eight-minute system for working with your money. As you review specific areas of your finances each week, the system helps you focus on each area of your money. Consider what you want to keep in your relationship and what you want to change with your finances. Celebrate your relationship by scheduling quality time with your money; choose the place for your weekly date with your money; and understand how to invest in your relationship each week so your money grows with you.

QUALITY TIME

Scheduling time in your busy schedule for your relationship with money is essential for your success with the DATING YOUR MONEY™ system. Check your calendar and pick a day to spend quality time with your money each week.

You may feel you already spend time with your money. Let's see: Take a look at how people choose to spend time with their money and see if any of the examples describes your relationship with your money:

The Flirt: You spend as little time as possible thinking about your finances each month because you're always chasing after new pursuits. You address the bare minimum in your financial life.

The One-Night Stand: You spend time with your money only at tax time. Once a year you hastily gather together whatever the accountant has requested. Then it's sayonara to your finances until next year. Long-term planning never comes up in your relationship with money.

The Arranged Marriage: Someone else manages your assets. Maybe it's a parent or a grandparent. Maybe you have married into your spouse's family money. Third parties set up your accounts, invest your cash, and balance your books.

The Chance Encounter: You wake up one day to find yourself in an awkward situation. You and your money are like two ships passing in the night. Whatever you learn about your financial situation comes as a great surprise.

Do any of these styles of money management provide the quality time and consistency critical to keeping your commitment to your relationship with money? When you are DATING YOUR MONEY™, the quality time you spend with your assets provides you with many opportunities for working with your finances so they don't become overwhelming.

To have an effective relationship in all areas of your money, please make a weekly date—same time, same day each week—when you spend at least eight minutes to meditate on your money. During this weekly session, you focus on nothing but your finances—for eight minutes. If the telephone rings, let it go to voice mail. Plan to eat before or after working with your money, because snacking is distracting. Now isolate yourself with your money so you can devote quality time to each other. Set an egg timer, digital alarm, or stop watch to eight minutes. Focus your thoughts on your money for the entire time, instead of thinking about how many minutes you have left!

On the other six days, spend a few minutes—five or less—to check in with your feelings about money: Pull out your MONEY MOOD METER™ and use it to measure your financial state of mind. Are you making progress on organizing your assets now that you are in touch with your feelings about money?

One last note on timing, your routine may be disrupted by events in your life. When you go on vacation, have guests, celebrate birthdays and holidays, enter tax season, etc., don't miss a beat. You may need to adjust your time to meditate on your money during these moments. However, be as consistent as possible about the time of your money date each week. Your money will thank you for it—and you will feel better supported by it.

A Space of One's Own

The space in which you work with your money is important. Before getting started on building your finances, select a location that has room for you to move around and a tabletop or flat surface to spread out your financial information. You'll need good light and power outlets for your computer equipment. In addition, have on hand pens, pencils, a sharpener, and a calculator. Think of everything you need in advance—all the paraphernalia for organizing your finances—so that you are successfully Dating Your Money™. For example, if you are high-tech, you will want to be wired to a computer and perhaps use other digital gadgets to get the job done. If you prefer hard copy, keep all account statements, checkbooks, bankbooks, and other financial records handy.

Now that you have arranged the space and time to bond with your finances, enjoy the process of Dating Your Money™. Get out your Money Mood Meter™ and measure your progress: How are you feeling these days about your money?

Dating Your Money™

The Dating Your Money™ system allows you to focus on each area of your money for eight minutes a week during a four-week cycle.

During the first month of practicing the system, it may take more than eight minutes each week to date your money successfully. Stay on target and before you know it, you'll be romancing your finances in less than eight minutes a week!

Are you feeling a bit ambivalent or anxious because eight minutes may not seem like enough time to connect with your money? Give yourself the opportunity to experience an eight-minute relationship, and you can make adjustments to the overall time once you find your own rhythm.

Keep your timer in a convenient place where you can see and hear it. Set it for eight minutes. If you wish to spend more time on the exercise, set the timer accordingly. Focus your thoughts on your money and the connection you want with it. Close your eyes, inhale and exhale slowly, and visualize enjoying a positive connection to money. Is your communication with money productive?

As you begin your weekly connection with your finances, create a special greeting of about thirty seconds to say each time you meet up with your money. Make it fun to be with your finances—so you work together effectively.

In four-week cycles, you synthesize the financial information you are compiling. Keep your economic research specific to the area that you're concentrating on so you can move efficiently from money subject to subject. Address one fiscal issue at a time. **Your finances are easier to understand when each area is broken out separately so you can evaluate it.**

Each week, focus on the various areas of your money— within eight minutes. Stay alert!

WEEK 1: EDUCATION AND PLAY

Begin each month with a positive perspective on how your money is helping you to grow and enjoy life. By focusing on how your money assists you in celebrating life, you make finance fun and money becomes supportive rather than a burden.

Look at the following areas in your life in which money plays a role in your growth and development:

Learning

Determine what you enjoy studying and learning in your life. Do you go to school? Do you attend workshops or seminars? Do you read books or use home-study courses? Identify what you are interested in learning more about. Are you enjoying fulfilling and fun educational experiences? Be aware of the costs of your education.

Playing

Play is what you do in your free time. Play is what you do when you feel free to do anything you desire—when time is endless and cost doesn't matter. Is this what it feels like to be financially free? What activities would you do if you were financially free? **Position your money so that it supports your interests and activities:** a day at an amusement park, a weekend skiing with friends, a walk on the beach, a big banana split shared with your family, or an intimate dinner with your sweetheart. Perhaps you have set aside money to take advantage of an unexpected opportunity or to make a serendipitous purchase.

Now think about where, when, and how often you like to play. Do you play enough or would you like to have more leisure time? Review the costs of play—include the activities you participate in and those you would like to add. Pinpoint areas in your financial life that you'd like to change. Would you like to increase opportunities for education and play?

Celebrate your accomplishments and your positive experiences with the money in your life. In your Money Dating Architecture™, you may want to create new structures, for example, starting a savings account to support hobbies and interests such as classes, earning a degree or certification, playing a sport, or getting bodywork or a massage once a month. Be decisive and position your cash so that it supports your activities. **Mantra: My money is always available for my personal growth and for new experiences.**

In some cases, you may feel you're not able to spend your money as if you were financially free. Take note of what you want to spend your money on and what it costs. Do research and comparison-shopping. Choose activities your money can support, so you celebrate what you have instead of regretting what you don't. When you appreciate the process of increasing your assets while enjoying what you have in the moment, you create momentum to reach even bigger goals.

Case in point: You want to travel on a cruise ship that stops in three Caribbean destinations. The trip costs more than you choose to spend right now on a vacation. Can you tailor your desires to fit your pocketbook? Do your research: Go to a travel agent or look on the Internet for affordable trips. Discover which cruise lines go to your desired destinations, where they leave from and when, and find out the costs for off-season travel and whether there are discount rates available.

If you are concerned about purchasing a vacation package at a particular time when money is scarce, tell yourself that the trip is the perfect destination and you are simply shopping around for the right price. **Be proactive:** Set aside a weekly amount of money for the cruise. Clip out pictures from magazines or catalogs of the destination, and display them prominently in your home to keep you focused on your goal.

In the meantime, enjoy your dream: Go to dinner in a Caribbean restaurant; buy a few items of clothing for the trip; purchase a travel guide for the destination and read up on your upcoming excursions. Every week, keep adding money to your vacation fund—add more than you planned if possible. Soon you'll be ready to purchase your dream vacation—you'll be cruising to the sunny Caribbean isles!

WEEK 2: BALANCE SHEET

This week your task is to review your income and your expenses for the past month. First, using your MONEY MOOD METER™ see how you are feeling about your income and expenditures.

Have your DATING YOUR MONEY W2 FORM™ from the past month available for a quick review. Include any information you have saved electronically with Quicken or Microsoft Money, or use your manual ledger and paper statements if you are working with hard copy. Your data is valuable because it provides information for your date with your money. Make sure all your financial information is within reach and that you reflect on how you feel during this date.

Ask the following questions while on your date with money this week:

What income has come in? Identify each source of income and the dates you received any monies. What have you spent? Have you spent more than you received, or did you earn more than you spent? What did you do with surplus income—did you put it in an interest bearing account, invest it in the market or in your business, buy art or collectibles, or spend it on yourself or others?

Think about how you answered the questions. Were you surprised by your answers? Did you receive the income you expected? Are you spending more or less than you thought? Is your money serving your best interests and providing you with the experiences you want in your life? Use your MONEY MOOD METER™ to evaluate your emotions while answering the questions.

What comes into and what flows out of your accounts? **Every relationship is a give-and-take exchange. When it comes to your money, giving and receiving are equally important concepts.**

What are your sources of income? Are you employed? Do you receive money that you don't have to work for? Passive income is the most effective way to produce cash while leveraging your time, effort, and energy. You are not working to provide the income—instead your money is working for you. Interest paid on your bank account and dividends paid on shares of stock are examples of passive income.

You may need to have a dialog with yourself for the full eight minutes. Think clearly; avoid emotional traps that paralyze your working successfully through your finances. You can always make another date with your money next week and pick up from where you left off before moving on to the next task!

If you are unhappy about the decisions you make about your relationship with money, take additional time during the week to look at your finances and make some new choices!

WEEK 3: CHARITY AND INVESTMENTS

Think about sharing your wealth. Review your financial architecture and how you are using your money, not only to invest in yourself but also to contribute to the world around you. **As the Chief Financial Officer (CFO) of your household, review how your money works for you—and how you are sharing it with those who are less fortunate.**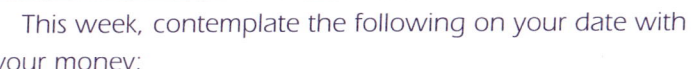

This week, contemplate the following on your date with your money:

Investments

What are your assets? Do you want to invest more of your money? Do your investments create adequate income? Are there other investments that you would like to know more about? Ask yourself about each of your investments: Is this investment choice making money for me?

Charity

Now let's take a look at the charities you donate to.
Look at how much of your money and time you give
to organizations. Are you passionate about how much
you are contributing? Would you like to give more to
your favorite causes? Are you satisfied with the
amounts of money that you give? Would you like to
adjust the amounts you donate and support additional
charitable organizations?

Here are some helpful hints to assist you with this
week's money activity:

When you receive your investment statements this month,
keep the information together for review during this week's
date. If you receive information electronically, organize it
in files and save it on your desktop for easy access. If you
receive information by mail and have hard copies, collect the
documents in a specific place and bring them on your date
with your money.

As you receive invitations to contribute to various charities,
create a folder to file these opportunities. Read about each
charity when you receive their information and ask: Do I
want to support this charity? Why do I want to support this
organization and how much would I like to donate? Make
notes about each group: write down or type in the charity
name, why you want to support it, and the amount you
would like to donate. (Post-it® Notes are perfect because their
size forces you to be brief.) Place a note with each charity
invitation that you are considering. Focus your giving on
charities that mean something to you as opposed to randomly

contributing to ones you are not passionate about. When you are ready to make your contributions (at the end of the year or quarterly), you will be prepared to follow your notes or "charity instructions." Streamlining the process of giving frees you to donate to charities you feel passionate about and puts your dollars to work more quickly for the organizations that matter to you.

WEEK 4: HOUSEHOLD CASH FLOW AND LONG-TERM SAVINGS

In week four you examine your personal money style. How do you pay for the products and services that support your lifestyle? Do you have long-term savings and investment strategies? During your date this week with your money, reflect on:

Payment Preference

When you are making a purchase, what form of payment do you typically reach for? Do you pull out your credit card or a debit card? Do you carry a lot of cash in your wallet? Do you like to write checks? What about online payments: Are you comfortable paying online? What is your method of choice for a payment?

Do you keep track of your spending? Do you consistently record where your money goes? Do you take your receipts from your purchases and keep them for tax purposes or other reasons? Do you make notes on the receipt to remind yourself which category this expense belongs in come tax time?

Savings

Reflect on your savings. Examine whether you are saving money, and review the amounts. Are you fulfilling your commitment to saving money? Do you make weekly deposits to your savings? How many savings accounts have you set up? You may want to open several savings accounts for different purposes and commit to weekly deposits for travel, home improvement, clothing, education, etc.

This week's assignment is: affirming different styles of working with money and reaching your savings goals. Honor your style of dealing with finances so that you succeed in all eight steps of DATING YOUR MONEY™.

By the end of the fourth week, you are ready to repeat the dating cycle. **Each month, you have the opportunity to review, evaluate, and build on the routines you have experienced during the four weeks.** After the initial thirty-day cycle, sit back for a moment and contemplate how you feel about your money. See whether your choices are working for you or against you. See how you have evolved, and make adjustments in your financial planning as you see fit.

LET'S PARTY

At the end of each date, congratulate yourself for your willingness to come into a relationship with your money! **Establish routines for yourself, preferably something physical like jumping in the air, shouting out loud, or throwing a party—do something that feels great at the end of your weekly date.** Feel good about dating your money over and over. Find a way to leave your date with a smile—knowing the joy of having money in your life to support you every step of the way.

HELPFUL HINTS

To keep the focus on your money, have financial information at your fingertips. File your financial data so you have it when you need it. Save your receipts each day not only for tax purposes (deductions) but also so you know where you spend your money. You want to record your income and expenditures every day.

At the end of each month if you have money left over, invest it. This money becomes a seed for change in your relationship to money because it may contribute toward creating a new source of income. Passive income is what you discover during the second week of each month while dating your money. **Because the seeds you plant are vital to your financial well-being, you determine how your money garden is growing.** As you make the right choices with money, you embrace interest-bearing investments because you have become financially intelligent. The practice of positioning your money makes all the difference in the world: You save, invest, enjoy your money—and see the results in the bank and in your life!

When you are DATING YOUR MONEY™, you become prosperous and fulfilled because you are not only financially savvy but also emotionally intelligent with your money. You are beginning to understand the essence of being a MONEY DATING ARCHITECT™—a person who builds money relationships that work for her!

Go to www.DatingYourMoney.com and celebrate your progress. You're moving ahead with your money at breakneck speed.

CHEERS TO YOU AND YOUR MONEY!

Chapter 7

DATING YOUR MONEY   PERSONALS   CH. 7: TAKING A MONEY TIME-OUT™

I need a vacation...

Looking for a
long-lasting
relationship
Looking for a
commitment
Looking for
a supportive
relationship
Looking for
a good
communicator
Looking for
someone easy
to spot in
a crowd
Looking for
someone who
knows what
they want from
life and is willing
to do whatever
it takes to get it
Looking for
someone to
grow with
I need a vacation...
Looking for
a good
communicator
Looking for
someone easy
to spot in
a crowd
Looking for
someone who
knows what
they want from

Looking for a
commitment
Looking for
a supportive
relationship
Looking for
a good
communicator
Looking for
someone easy
to spot in
a crowd
I need a vacation!
Looking for
someone to
grow with
Looking for a
commitment
Looking for
a supportive
relationship
Looking for
a good
communicator
Looking for
someone easy
to spot in
a crowd
Looking for
someone who
knows what
they want from
life and is willing
to do whatever
it takes to get it
Looking for
someone to

someone easy
to spot in
a crowd
Looking for
someone who
knows what
they want from
life and is willing
to do whatever
it takes to get it
Looking for
someone to
grow with
Looking for a
long-lasting
relationship
Looking for a
commitment
Looking for
a supportive
relationship
Looking for
a good
communicator
Looking for
someone easy
to spot in
a crowd
I need a vacation...
Looking for
someone to
grow with
Looking for a

to do whatever
it takes to get it
Looking for
someone to
grow with
Looking for a
commitment
Looking for
a supportive
relationship
Looking for
a good
communicator
Looking for
someone easy
to spot in
a crowd
Looking for
someone who
knows what
they want from
life and is willing
to do whatever
it takes to get it
Looking for a
long-lasting
relationship
Looking for a
commitment
Looking for
a supportive
relationship

is willing
to do whatever
it takes to get it
Embracing
Change
Looking for a
long-lasting
relationship
Looking for a
commitment
Looking for
a supportive
relationship
Looking for
a good
communicator
Looking for
someone easy
to spot in
a crowd
Looking for
someone who
knows what
they want from
Looking for a
long-lasting
relationship
Looking for a
commitment
Looking for
a supportive
relationship
Looking for

Looking for a
long-lasting
relationship
Looking for a
commitment
Looking for
a supportive
relationship
Looking for
a good
communicator
Looking for
someone easy
to spot in
a crowd
Looking for
someone who
knows what
they want from
life and is willing
to do whatever
it takes to get it
Looking for
someone to
grow with
Looking for a
long-lasting
relationship
Looking for a
commitment
Looking for
a supportive
relationship
I need a vacation...
Looking for
someone easy
to spot in

I need a vacation from my money...

Taking a
Money Time-Out™

You've got the recipe for financial success—and you and your money are finally in a groove! You know how to access your financial resources, so study your options. Your finances are well organized, and you are on time for your weekly eight-minute date with your money. Are you enjoying DATING YOUR MONEY™ yet?

Some money relationships start off running—they are full of spark, excitement, and delight. You feel inspired and energized when you are with your money. But after a few weeks, you begin to feel uncomfortable and a quiet distance settles in between you and your money. Your interest level in the subject of finances wanes. Your relationship with your money drifts, and you're not sure what to do about it. How do you keep the relationship alive? How do you get back on track with your cash so that DATING YOUR MONEY™ is exciting and fun again?

In the seventh step of DATING YOUR MONEY™, you learn acceptance in your financial life. You give space to your relationship with money. Effectively using time to gain perspective and returning to the relationship with a clear head and without guilt, you seize opportunities for breaks from your day-to-day finances and seek guidance when you reach a stalemate with your money. Taking a MONEY TIME-OUT™ is the best way to build a relationship with your money because giving space allows you and your money room for growth.

"I need a break…"

What Is a Money Time-Out™?

People often lose their desire to spend time, energy, and effort with their money. Everybody reaches a point where she needs a break in the routine for a chance to breathe. Who doesn't crave the opportunity to get away from money? Because of the enormous investment of time and energy, many people grow tired—it seems all they need is a break from their schedules to be able to return to dating their money with more love and appreciation in their hearts.

Think about how the following stories relate to your relationship with money.

The folks in these examples live in the real world and are dealing with real-life time-outs:

Julie is a basketball player and enjoys playing on a team. During games, teams request time-outs—which the referee grants. The teams are aware that although time is being taken away from playing time—the time is used constructively for refocusing and regrouping. Based on what the team members have experienced and learned during the game, they come back to the court with renewed spirit and a game plan. Time-outs have a beginning and an end, and often allow teams to make a comeback in the next segment of the game. At the end of a time-out, a team literally jumps back into the game because the process of taking a break is revitalizing.

Another example of successful time-outs is how we work with our children when they're out of control. When children in school or at home are behaving wildly, adults offer time-outs as a means of controlling the immediate problem. The child has a chance to stop acting out, breathe, and calm down. The time-out has a beginning and end. When the time-out is over, both child and adult come back to the relationship with a different perspective.

Can you apply the lessons in real-life time-outs to your relationship with your money? You may find that you "need space" with your money too. Do you want to get as far away from your money as possible? Do you care whether or not you come back to your money? Do you need some time away from working on your finances to gain perspective?

Admittedly your relationship with money is one of the most intense partnerships you'll ever have. Understanding how to take a MONEY TIME-OUT™ is critical for your long-term success, so let's explore further how this works…

CALLING A TIME-OUT

A MONEY TIME-OUT™ begins with an acknowledgment that you need space and some distance from your money. One indication that you are losing interest in the subject is inconsistency in your DATING YOUR MONEY™ schedule. Slowly but surely you lose sight of the work you've been doing with your money.

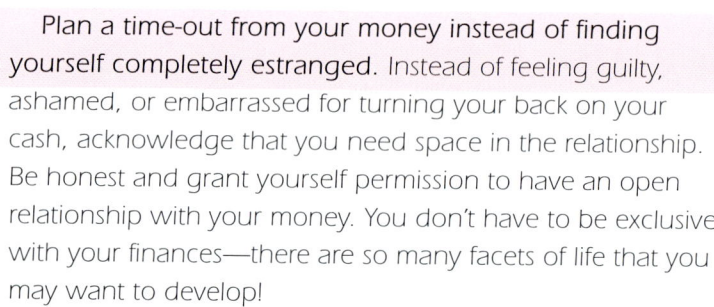

Plan a time-out from your money instead of finding yourself completely estranged. Instead of feeling guilty, ashamed, or embarrassed for turning your back on your cash, acknowledge that you need space in the relationship. Be honest and grant yourself permission to have an open relationship with your money. You don't have to be exclusive with your finances—there are so many facets of life that you may want to develop!

Allowing yourself to take a vacation or holiday from your money relationship, you automatically release a lot of pent-up emotions. Repeat this affirmation, if necessary: I am entitled to take a time-out. It is essential for my personal growth with my money. **Remember: You come first in your money relationship. Grant yourself a time-out when you feel you need it.**

LEAVING YOUR MONEY

When you are ready for a MONEY TIME-OUT™, you decide when to leave, how much time you will spend away, and when you will return to the relationship.

In the real world when one person leaves a relationship, the partner asks: "Why are you leaving? When are you coming back?" Sometimes a person leaves for good. Money, for better or worse, is not going anywhere. You can't love and then leave your money—you're stuck with each other. Get used to the marriage with your money—and learn to take breaks. Because all work and no play with money makes for a very dull life indeed! So after you've decided to hitch out of town, remember that you're leaving temporarily—and your return is critical to your overall financial success. **Plan your MONEY TIME-OUT™: Come back reenergized and ready to dig your heels in.**

MONEY TIME-OUT™ REVEALED

Think about why you need a time-out: Is there something in your financial relationship particularly challenging, boring, or confusing? What triggered your desire for space?

Let's look at a practical application for taking a Money Time-Out™. When your financial statements arrive with an error or the balance differs from what you have calculated, do you feel frustrated and discouraged because you have been diligently Dating Your Money™ for several weeks? Do you want to give up working with your money?

Understanding why you want to take a time-out from your relationship with your money is key to your comeback. Resolving your reasons for the break and then plotting your return to the game, you move forward—fast.

Your emotions surface again and again—influencing not only the choices you make about your money but also your feelings about taking a Money Time-Out™. How do you feel about taking a break from your money? This is a perfect time to get out your Money Mood Meter™ and check in. Being clear about each Money Time-Out™ you take is important to your staying in the game—and being a player in your financial life.

Timing is important in dating—being at the right place at the right time to meet the right person. How does this apply to having a successful relationship with your money?

Timing—like a time-out—also involves a beginning and an ending. When you begin the process of sorting out your finances, you are alone—separate and apart from your money. After many weeks of Dating Your Money™ you may feel that familiarity breeds contempt. So give yourself a reasonable break. We are not talking about a year—just enough time for some space, without losing your connection to the work that you've begun. Follow-through is required—to get results, see the process to the end.

My recommendation for a MONEY TIME-OUT™ is twenty-four to forty-eight hours, maximum—time to breathe without losing touch with your money. Staying the course of the DATING YOUR MONEY™ system means knowing when you will return to your practice. Running away from your money won't get you any closer to your dreams or living life easily; it will make working with your money harder and more challenging.

The MONEY TIME-OUT™ is used for you to reflect on what you really want out of your relationship with money. During your time-out, take the time to analyze how you work with your money. Do you enjoy meeting up and spending time with your finances? Think about areas in your financial life in which your money is not working for you. When are the times you dread showing up to be with your money? Which dates with your money do you show up late for or skip all together? Also, do you ever push away people who would like to assist you with your money?

At the beginning of a MONEY TIME-OUT™, declare why you need time away and decide how long you will take a break. Identify what you find challenging in your relationship with your money and what you want to change. At the end of your MONEY TIME-OUT™, ask whether you have accomplished your goal: Do you feel refreshed and ready to get back to work on your financial planning? Do you need a longer vacation from your money?

Use your MONEY MOOD METER™ and check in with your feelings. Let the

I take a MONEY TIME-OUT™ and stay connected to the relationship.

THE MONEY MOOD METER™

Ecstatic
Elated
Prosperous

Delighted
Blessed
Joyful

Cheerful
Happy
Pleased

Encouraged
Purposeful
Determined

Anxious
Confused
Concerned

Worried
Disturbed
Depressed

Disappointed
Disillusioned
Defeated

Frustrated
Upset
Angry

MONEY MOOD METER™ give you clues about whether you need more space or if you're ready to be on task.

The MONEY TIME-OUT™ is a tool to be used as needed in the DATING YOUR MONEY™ system to help you reach your financial goals. As you get more involved each week, you are working on—instead of passively being in—a relationship with your money. Taking charge of your finances means positioning your money so it can support anything your heart desires.

CAN I AFFORD THIS?

You may be wondering if you can afford to take a MONEY TIME-OUT™. Great question! The answer is you can't afford not to take a break—because the time-out is what gets you in gear for the final step: becoming a MONEY DATING ARCHITECT™. At this stage of the game, a MONEY TIME-OUT™ helps you create a plan and strategy to keep your relationship with your money running smoothly.

Money task: During your money break think about what you want in your financial life. Visualize it. Before your twenty-four- to forty-eight-hour money break, identify the amount of money required for your lifestyle during this period. Tack on an extra 10 percent to this number to cover any unexpected expenses during your time away. To spend your money satisfyingly based on your action plan, identify approximately the assets you need to support your dreams and reflect on the monies you earn, have saved and invested. Review your DATING YOUR MONEY W2 FORM™ balance sheet—and take a sharp look at the figures. Think about your budget during MONEY TIME-OUT™ cycles—and feel free to adjust the numbers later on to reflect your needs.

WRITE IT DOWN

When you have come back from your MONEY TIME-OUT™, write down any insights you had on the break. To assist you with recording your conclusions, go to www.DatingYourMoney.com and download the MONEY TIME-OUT™ worksheet. The form guides you through your writing about experiences and feelings before and after a time-out.

FINAL WORDS ABOUT KEEPING COMMITMENTS

A MONEY TIME-OUT™ is the best way to keep commitments to yourself and your money. During your break, reflect on commitments that you have made: Are you keeping them?

Do you want to keep the commitments you have made—or make new ones in your financial life? Change your commitments as you see fit: Make sure they are up-to-date with your goals. Ask yourself: How can my money better support me today and in the future?

Renewing your commitments to money jump-starts your future plans. In the same way a married couple renews their vows, you reaffirm your relationship with your money. Sustaining the spark in your relationship, you and your money look forward to greater opportunities.

Change your relationships—including your relationship with your money—and you change your life. As you change and grow as a person, your life grows and changes too. Ask yourself: What do I enjoy and what don't I like in my life? Can I sustain a relationship with my money so that I realize both my personal and financial goals?

Go to www.DatingYourMoney.com and cozy up with your finances… You are forever evolving in your extraordinary money relationship.

OUTSTANDING!

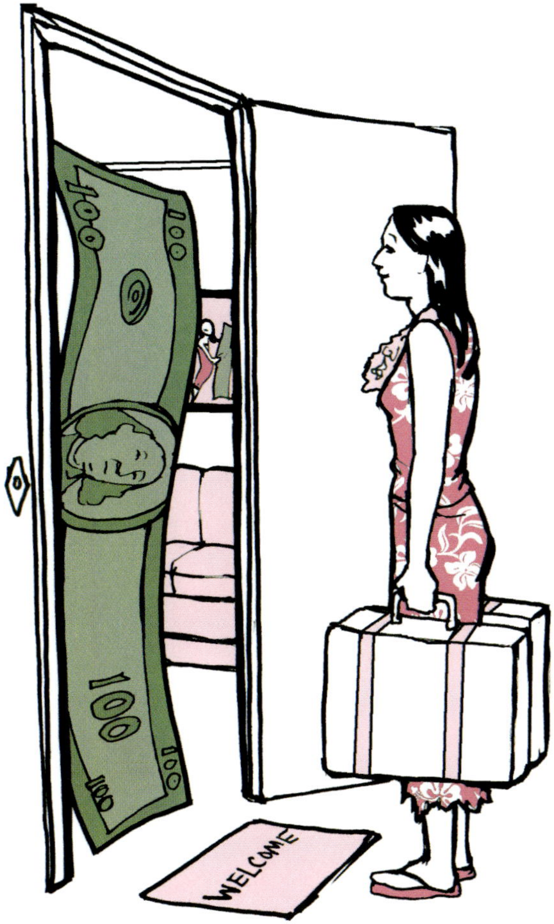

"It's great to have you back
in my life again..."

Chapter 8

Looking for someone to grow with...

Looking for a long-lasting relationship

Looking for a commitment

Looking for a supportive relationship

Looking for a good communicator

Looking for someone easy to spot in a crowd.

Looking for someone who knows what they want from life and is willing to do whatever it takes to get

Looking for someone to grow with.

I need a vacation.

Looking for a good communicator

Looking for someone easy to spot in a crowd.

Looking for someone who knows what they want from

Looking for a commitment

Looking for a supportive relationship

Looking for a good communicator

Looking for someone to spot in a crowd.

I need a vacation.

Looking for someone to grow with

Looking for a supportive relationship

Looking for a good communicator

Looking for someone easy to spot in a crowd.

Looking for someone who knows what they want from life and is willing to do whatever it takes to get it.

Looking for someone to grow with

Looking for a

Looking for someone who knows what they want from life and is willing to do whatever it takes to get it.

Embracing change

Looking for a long-lasting relationship

Looking for a commitment

Looking for a supportive relationship

Looking for a good communicator

Looking for someone easy to spot in a crowd.

Looking for someone who knows what they want from

Looking for a long-lasting relationship

Looking for a commitment

Looking for a supportive relationship

Looking for

Looking for someone who knows what they want from life and is willing to do whatever it takes to get it

Looking for a long-lasting relationship

Looking for a commitment

Looking for a supportive relationship

Looking for a good communicator

Looking for someone easy to spot in a crowd.

Looking for someone who knows what they want from life and is willing to do whatever it takes to get it

Looking for someone to grow with

Looking for a long-lasting relationship

Looking for a commitment

Looking for a supportive relationship

I need a vacation...

Looking for someone easy to spot in.

What's next?
Lots of continued growth!

Embracing Change

The sun sets in the west; it's the end of another glorious day. The evening feels different—a calm settles in. Because you have changed—your relationship with money is flourishing. Your money is providing opportunities for you to grow and change. You have let go of unsupportive money habits, and have made choices about your relationship with money based on your desires and research.

You have learned so much in the seven steps that I'd like to enumerate your accomplishments. You have made a commitment to your finances that you know how to keep. You celebrate when money flows freely in your life and you work on the areas in your financial life that need fixing. Because you know that money is supercharged with emotions, you turn to the MONEY MOOD METER™ as a quick fix when you are sorting out your feelings about your finances. Honoring your emotions while keeping your commitment to the relationship with your money, you remain true to yourself. Bravo!

Don't be shy—please congratulate yourself. You have identified your MONEY CONNECTION STYLE™ and have your own financial language down pat so that you communicate easily with your money. You track your money and have a deeper understanding of how you invest, save, donate, and shop. You spend quality time with your finances and know when to take a MONEY TIME-OUT™ to get a fresh perspective on growing with your money.

Shall I say more? You love what you do for your money, and you love what it does for you.

Learning new information while sustaining your relationship with money is easier than ever. Fulfilling a lifelong dream of having a positive relationship with your money is yours simply by DATING YOUR MONEY™. In this eighth and final step of DATING YOUR MONEY™, you continue the growth process, evolve with your finances, and embrace…change.

THE NATURE OF CHANGE

Your life changes every day, including activities you engage in, your energy level, efforts you make, and the time available to you. Shedding experiences that you no longer have an interest in, you absorb information and interact more joyfully in the world around you.

When building a relationship with money in the eighth and final step, you need to accept that who you are today is not who you will be in one month, six months, twelve months, or more. Learning expands your perception of the world as well as the perception of your money and how your finances best work for you. As you continue to communicate with your money, inform it of your changing needs and desires.

Question: Before exploring the DATING YOUR MONEY™ system, were you fully aware of your relationship with money? Now that you have read DATING YOUR MONEY™ and worked on the exercises, do you have a different perspective on money and your relationship with it?

In completing the weekly exercises in DATING YOUR MONEY™, **you connect not only with your money but also with yourself.** Do you have a better understanding of changes you want to make with your money? Cultivating a relationship with your money means being consistent in your communication and encouraging... change.

A LONG-LASTING RELATIONSHIP

The choices you make about your money nourish the relationship. When you are DATING YOUR MONEY™, you are informing your finances of the changes you want for yourself and your money. **As you change, position your finances so they support you. Without your input, your finances have no idea what they are doing—you guide your money.**

Think about it: If you do what you always do, you'll get what you always get. Do your homework to make informed decisions about money. Chances are you outgrow your money as you become more competent in organizing it. As a MONEY DATING ARCHITECT™, you are responsible for using the system's tools to keep your finances vibrant and healthy. **Remember you're in charge—this is a secret to maintaining a long-lasting relationship with your money.** As you continue DATING YOUR MONEY™, include experts in your money dialogue. Be clear and let them know how you talk shop. As your financial acumen increases, your money will follow your lead to financial freedom. **Now that you know how to love your money, let it love you back.**

You have accomplished all eight steps for DATING YOUR MONEY™! As a full-fledged MONEY DATING ARCHITECT™, go to www.DatingYourMoney.com.

Congratulations! How do you feel?

Epilogue

As I sit here writing some final thoughts, I'd like to say that I am delighted about your new relationship with your money!

You have opened yourself up to a new way of thinking about finances. Through the DATING YOUR MONEY™ system, you have let go of your past routines with money and bravely ventured into the unknown—a place where you need to create and redefine your relationship to money. Keep what is making you happy, change what is no longer contributing to your well-being, and understand that people change— as does your relationship to finances.

You are at an important crossroad: lead with your needs, or lead with your dreams.

The DATING YOUR MONEY™ system is a gift that changes people's lives. As you know, when your relationship with your money changes—everything changes. When your finances make a positive contribution to your life, you feel the benefits: financial freedom and personal growth.

Once you have created a warm, loving relationship with your money, you have a new language with which to communicate about your finances and a unique opportunity to make a money connection. Let others in your life know that they can change their relationship with their money too. Share the information in this book with others and pay it forward. Show a loved one, colleague, or friend your MONEY MOOD METER™ and ask how they feel about their money. Refer information seekers to www.DatingYourMoney.com to find out more.

Thank yourself for your willingness to keep your commitment to Dᴀᴛɪɴɢ Yᴏᴜʀ Mᴏɴᴇʏ™. Acknowledge your achievement. Recognize that you have chosen to spend your time, energy, effort—and money—on this investment in your own personal growth and development.

Congratulations on your completion of all eight steps of the Dᴀᴛɪɴɢ Yᴏᴜʀ Mᴏɴᴇʏ™ system. Go to www.DatingYourMoney.com and print out your MDA™ certificate and celebrate your success. Display the certificate in your home or office because it is a reminder that you are building a long-lasting money relationship and are well on your way to becoming a Mᴏɴᴇʏ Dᴀᴛɪɴɢ Aʀᴄʜɪᴛᴇᴄᴛ™.

With great joy, I commend your ongoing progress: Be well and be prosperous!

About the Author
Jennifer S. Wilkov, CFP®

An expert in strategic planning and business development across the nation's top companies, and a Certified Financial Planner™, Jennifer S. Wilkov has over a decade of experience with money relationships—both corporate and individual. Her company, Evolutionary Strategic Planning (E.S.P.), provides a unique approach to working with clients based on their key needs and desires. As a financial **pioneer**, she has helped clients design strategies and create multiple income streams so they can swiftly reach their financial goals.

It's no accident that the acronym for her company is E.S.P. Her clients agree: she has a sixth sense! Collaborating with Jennifer means forming an alliance—Jennifer remains with clients as they evolve, update, and revise their financial plans, making sure that as they grow, their wealth grows with them.

Finally, as author and speaker, Jennifer brings her many years of knowledge and wisdom to the table to show you just how easy it is to love your money and to love what it does for you.

DATING YOUR MONEY™

DATING YOUR MONEY	PERSONALS	RECOMMENDED RESOURCES

How do I get more support?

Looking for a long-lasting relationship
Looking for a commitment
Looking for a supportive relationship
Looking for a good communicator
How do I get more support?
Looking for someone who knows what they want from life and is willing to do whatever it takes to get it.
Looking for someone to grow with
I need a vacation!
Looking for a good communicator
Looking for someone easy to spot in a crowd.
Looking for someone who knows what they want from life and is willing

Looking for a supportive relationship
Looking for a good communicator
Looking for someone to grow with
Looking for a commitment
Looking for a supportive relationship
Looking for a good communicator
Looking for someone easy to spot in a crowd.
Looking for someone who knows what they want from life and is willing to do whatever it takes to get it.
Looking for someone to grow with
Looking for a commitment

they want from life and is willing to do whatever it takes to get it.
Looking for someone to grow with
Looking for a long-lasting relationship
Looking for a commitment
Looking for a supportive relationship
Looking for a good communicator
Looking for someone easy to spot in a crowd
I need a vacation!
Looking for someone to grow with
Looking for a commitment

Looking for a long-lasting relationship
Looking for a supportive relationship
Looking for a good communicator
Looking for someone easy to spot in a crowd
Looking for someone who knows what they want from life and is willing to do whatever it takes to get it
Looking for a long-lasting relationship
Looking for a commitment
Looking for a supportive relationship
Looking for a good

relationship
Looking for a commitment
Looking for a supportive relationship
Looking for a good communicator
Looking for someone easy to spot in a crowd
Looking for someone who knows what they want from life and is willing to do whatever it takes to get it
Looking for someone to grow with
Looking for a long-lasting relationship
Looking for a commitment
Looking for a supportive relationship
Looking for someone easy to spot in

I can have a relationship in 8 minutes a week?

Recommended Resources

Dating Your Money™
♥ Newsletter ♥

Each month

I share insights and information on how to enhance your relationship with your money and what to focus on in your financial life.

Learn

DATING YOUR MONEY™ strategies so you and your money grow. I am delighted to be on your championship team and support you in developing your relationship every month of the year!

Sign up

for the DATING YOUR MONEY™ newsletter at www.DatingYourMoney.com

The MONEY MOOD METER™

Become aware of what you are feeling when any financial situation comes up!

Ask yourself: "How do I feel about my money **right now**?"

AND KEEP IT CLOSE TO YOUR…

Bills ▪ Cash ▪ Credit Cards
Checkbook ▪ Investments

USE THE MONEY MOOD METER™ EVERY TIME YOU MEET YOUR MONEY!

Share the wealth…

Makes a great gift for family, friends, and colleagues!

TO **LEARN MORE,** GO TO
WWW.DATINGYOURMONEY.COM

THE MONEY MOOD METER™

Ecstatic Elated Prosperous
Delighted Blessed Joyful
Cheerful Happy Pleased
Encouraged Purposeful Determined
Anxious Confused Concerned
Worried Disturbed Depressed
Disappointed Disillusioned Defeated
Frustrated Upset Angry

SPEAKING ENGAGEMENTS

Jennifer S. Wilkov, CFP®, is one of the most sought-after female speakers on money relationships and living life to its fullest.

Her unique approach to combining emotional intelligence with financial wisdom provides audiences with an extraordinary experience of insight and knowledge, as well as a concrete plan for their money.

Jennifer's enthusiastic presentation of information about money and finances inspires audiences everywhere.

To have **Jennifer S. Wilkov**, CFP®,
appear at your next event,
e-mail info@GetMyESP.com
or call 1-877-6GET-ESP.

Once you **enjoy** your relationship with your money, you're ready to **join** your finances with a soul mate!

Learn how to love your money as a couple in...

DATING YOUR MONEY FOR COUPLES!

AVAILABLE
Valentine's Day 2007

❤

Love what you do for your money...
and Love what it does for you!